THE CASANOVA FABLE

THE DOCTOR'S TABLE

THE CASANOVA FABLE

A SATIRICAL REVALUATION

BY

WILLIAM GERHARDI
&
HUGH KINGSMILL

ILLUSTRATED
BY
P. YOUNGMAN
CARTER

JARROLDS PUBLISHERS LONDON
LIMITED, 34 PATERNOSTER ROW E.C.4
MCMXXXIV

2.855

Made and Printed by Litho Offset in Great Britain at
GREYCAINES
(Taylor Garnett Evans & Co. Ltd.)
Watford, Herts.

CONTENTS

PART ONE

THE EVIDENCE

PAGE

INTRODUCTION. CASANOVA'S VERACITY . . 11

CHAPTER

I. FIRST JOURNEY INTO THE WORLD . . . 20

II. SOME MISHAPS AND A VENETIAN SENATOR . 36

III. HENRIETTE—CASANOVA'S GREAT LOVE . . 47

IV. THE TWO NUNS, AND THE ESCAPE FROM THE
LEADS 60

V. THE MARCHIONESS D'URFÉ 80

VI. SORCERY 92

VII. LONDON AND LA CHARPILLON . . . 105

VIII. THE LAW'S DESPATCH 121

IX. THE DEATH OF A CHRISTIAN . . . 141

PART TWO

THE SUMMING-UP 165

LIST OF ILLUSTRATIONS

FRONTISPIECE

FACING PAGE

GIACOMO CASANOVA 32

" VENICE IN THE EIGHTEENTH CENTURY NO LONGER
RANKED AMONG THE GREAT POWERS OF EUROPE " . 64

" A VIOLENT STORM BROKE OUT AS HE WAS MAKING HIS
INCANTATIONS " 96

" HENRIETTE WAS DRESSED AS AN OFFICER IN A BLUE
UNIFORM " 128

" IN LOVE MEN AND WOMEN FOR THE MOST PART DUPE
EACH OTHER " 160

" AT MY AGE I WAS PREPARED FOR DISLOYALTY IN A
WOMAN " 176

" IN A FIT OF HOMESICKNESS HE RETURNED " . . 208

PART ONE

THE EVIDENCE

INTRODUCTION

CASANOVA died in 1798, at the age of seventy-three, leaving behind him in the castle at Dux, where in his last years he had been librarian to Count Waldstein, twelve volumes of memoirs, entitled *Histoire de ma Vie jusqu'à l'an* 1797. More than twenty years after Casanova's death, a man called Carlo Angiolini brought this manuscript to the famous Leipzig publisher, Brockhaus, who issued a German translation of it between 1822 and 1828. This version, which reproduced the original in a much expurgated form, was translated into French. A few years later, Brockhaus, wishing for a more faithful version of the original than either the German or French one, commissioned a Monsieur Laforgue, professor of French at Dresden, to bring out a new edition of the original manuscript. Monsieur Laforgue undertook the task, but being entirely out of sympathy with Casanova, emended and expurgated him still more extensively than his predecessors. Thus, within forty years of Casanova's death, three versions of his Memoirs appeared, the last of which differed so much from its predecessors as to provoke a natural doubt both about the existence of an original manuscript, and about the existence of Casanova himself.

This doubt persisted until the last quarter of the nineteenth century, and was strengthened by the spirit of the age, which regarded the great or notorious figures of the past with suspicion. Homer, during this period, melted into a mob of itinerant ballad-mongers, Christ became a solar myth, and Shakespeare became Bacon. That nothing had happened as it was reported to have happened, and that anyone whose existence could not be disproved must have been somebody else, were the two main assumptions of the age which created scientific history. In such an atmosphere Casanova was a lost man. His existence was denied, and his Memoirs, declared to be a work of fiction, were attributed to various authors, the most favoured being the sophisticated Stendhal, who could no more have written Casanova's Memoirs than Joseph Conrad could have written *Midshipman Easy*.

The rehabilitation of Casanova was begun round about 1880, and the labours of Monsieur Armand Baschet, of Signor Alessandro d'Ancona, of Herr F. W. Barthold, Mr. Arthur Symons, Dr. Guède, Dr. Tage Bull, and many others restored Casanova to reality, and the Memoirs to Casanova.

In the first enthusiasm of discovering that Casanova was not a myth, some of his admirers went too far in the opposite direction. The fact that a number of contemporary references to him, chiefly in police archives, had been unearthed certainly proved that he was a real man, but did not guarantee his veracity. In 1755, to give one example, a spy attached to the Venetian Inquisition reported to his employers that Casanova united impiety, imposture, and wantonness to a degree that inspired horror. Not all the references unearthed were as disparaging as this, but none of them justified the ardour with which Havelock Ellis wrote of Casanova's truthfulness in an essay first published in 1898. " So far as investigation has yet been able to go," Havelock Ellis said, " he wrote with strict regard to truth. Whenever it is possible to test Casanova, his essential veracity has always been vindicated. . . . When we remember that he was telling the story of his life primarily for his own pleasure, it is clear that he had no motive for deception."

Nearly twenty years later, in a preface to a new edition of the book containing his essay on Casanova, Havelock Ellis wrote of Casanova's veracity in a more guarded tone, withdrawing the " undisputed credit " he had previously allowed to the Memoirs. " We cannot take for granted," he said, " that he exerted in the narration of his life a scrupulosity which, on his own showing, he failed to exert in the living of it. Numerous details of the narrative cannot be verified where we should expect them to be verified ; various episodes have, rightly or wrongly, been regarded by some critics as imaginary interpolations. . . ."

The mildly sceptical attitude here suggested is the one taken in the present study. In dealing with a man like Casanova who, though of immense importance to himself, did not distinguish himself sufficiently either in action or in literature to be portrayed in detail by his contemporaries, one can test the veracity of his self-portrait only by the consistency of its various parts with one another, and with the impression of Casanova gained from his Memoirs as a whole. Such a test does not possess what pedants call " objective validity," but may be none the less effective for that.

Even if there were any reason to believe that Casanova was naturally truthful, the circumstances in which he wrote his Memoirs were unfavourable to an accurate transcription of his past. For the last fourteen years of his life, from fifty-nine to seventy-three, he lived, with a few interruptions, at Dux in Bohemia as the librarian of Count Waldstein. He had met the young Count by chance, and learnt that he was interested in the occult sciences. This was a subject on which Casanova spoke with authority, for he had made more money out of the occult sciences than out of any other single activity. The Count was fascinated, and invited Casanova to stay with him.

The invitation was terminated only by Casanova's death, fourteen years later. But the glamour of his guest soon faded for the Count ; and in the last seven years or so, the period during which Casanova was compiling his Memoirs, the librarian of Dux was not taken seriously either by the Count, his guests, or the domestic staff. He began to see slights everywhere : the soup is served too hot so as to annoy him, the others are handed the strawberries before he is, the parish priest thinks him in need of conversion, his stately bow, relic of a politer age, moves his boorish companions to laughter, he treads the minuet before louts to whom the elegance of the world destroyed by the French Revolution is a subject for merriment, and, crowning blow, one day he finds his portrait nailed to the door of the privy.

But worse than these slights to his vanity from the outer world was the ennui which consumed every hour of his waking life. Although, according to the Prince de Ligne, Count Waldstein's uncle, Casanova quoted Homer and Horace *ad nauseam* in his old age, the pleasures of the mind meant little to him. To impose himself on others had always been his ruling passion, and if he quoted Homer and Horace it was rather to annoy his audience than to raise himself above the will. A parade of erudition was all that was left to the old man who had conquered so many women and outwitted so many men; that, and the pleasures of the table. But towards the close even his appetite left him.

The more complex appetite of love had left him some years earlier, and it was this loss which oppressed him most. The pleasures of the table gratified only his body, but the pleasures of love had thrilled his whole being. " The chief occupation of my life," he says in the preface to the Memoirs, " has been to cultivate the pleasures of the senses. Nothing has ever meant as much to me as that. Feeling myself born for the fair sex, I have always loved it, and have been loved in return as often as possible. I have also always had a great liking for good cheer."

This linking of food with women suggests that the gratification of his senses was only less important to Casanova than the gratification of his vanity. Elsewhere in the preface, he passes without any softening transition from his passion for old cheese to the pleasant fragrance of the women he has loved. Being exceptionally vigorous and full-blooded, physical enjoyment was proportionately valued by him ; and if the choice between a beautiful woman whose favours had to be purchased, and a somewhat less beautiful woman who was offering herself from love, had been placed before him, one cannot say whether his vanity or his senses would have won. Probably he would have chosen the venal beauty and appeased his self-love by refusing to pay her afterwards.

Deprived in his last years of everything which had made life pleasurable to his senses and gratifying to his vanity, the past was his only refuge from the mortifications of the present, and the inducement to omit from his record anything which could wound his self-love, and to embellish it with imaginary incidents of a romantic kind, was therefore much stronger than if he had begun his autobiography in earlier more prosperous days. Fortunately, however, for the interest and comparative credibility of his record, his self-love was not of a squeamish kind, nor did his high opinion of his own virtue require that he should suppress the recollection of how he had swindled one person, or revenged himself on another. In the bitterness of his old age the thought of how he had made others suffer afforded him in some moods great satisfaction. He even speaks somewhere of the " cynicism " of his Memoirs. But his cynicism seldom comes to the surface. " I examined my conduct, and found it irreproachable," is his usual attitude towards such actions of his as may be open to misconstruction.

In the preface to his Memoirs he runs lightly over the various charges which unintelligent persons might bring against him. As to the deceit he has perpetrated upon women, let it pass, he says. Men and women dupe each other in love. The point is not worth dwelling upon. But the fools he has parted from their money are another matter. " One avenges intellect when one dupes a fool." It almost amounts to a duty. Many of his friends, he admits, were among his dupes, but in emptying their purses he conferred a double benefit on them. In the first place, he taught them the wisdom which springs from disillusionment ; he cured them of idle dreams. And in the second place he applied to his own enjoyment money which they would have wasted on extravagant follies. It was not as if he had hoarded the sums he received from them. " I might consider myself guilty, were I rich to-day," he says. " But I have nothing. I have thrown it all away. That is my consolation ; that is my defence."

The fact that his affections were neither deep nor

long-lived he also explains to his own satisfaction. "I was always cheerful," he says, "always ready to pass from one pleasure to another.. . . . . Hence, no doubt, my tendency to make new acquaintances, and my facility in breaking with them, although always for a sound reason, and never in mere levity."

Encouraged by discovering that he is free from levity, he goes a step further and affirms that he is not sensual : "To call me sensual would be a mistake, for my desires, however vehement, have never made me neglect such duties as I had "—a statement which does not appear to mean much more than that he did not allow his affairs with women to distract him from depriving his friends and acquaintances of their money.

Naturally he adds veracity to his other virtues. He is anxious, he says, that his work shall contain the truth and nothing but the truth, and the judgment of the learned and reflective, he believes, will be in favour of his veracity, since he is writing chiefly for his own pleasure, and no man can have any object in deceiving himself : a poor argument from whichever side one regards it. In the first place his appeal to the learned and reflective shows that he is writing to convince others as well as to please himself ; and secondly a large measure of self-deception is for most men, and certainly was for Casanova, an essential preliminary to an easy mind.

All these protestations show that Casanova was not, as some of his admirers have painted him, the completely natural man, recording his life without moral embarrassment. The completely natural man, untroubled by moral aspirations, is a mythical creature. Virtue is an object of desire, as much as women and money. But Casanova was too impulsive and simple-minded to be mastered by a senile preoccupation with virtue. As far as one can judge, he seldom suppresses or transforms his actions in the interests of his moral reputation, but contents himself with denying that they were as reprehensible as an unintelligent person might suppose. His Memoirs, to sum up, are not misleading through failing to reveal what he did, but through the addition of imaginary embellishments. Casanova, had he quarrelled with a prostitute, knocked her down, and gone off with her purse, would have narrated the incident without a qualm, but a vague feeling that a little glamour was needed to round the story off would have made him introduce a lovely young countess designed by art and nature to make a man forget the small unpleasantnesses of life.

CHAPTER ONE

GIACOMO CASANOVA, the eldest of a family of six, was born in Venice on April 2, 1725. His father was an actor, and his mother, the daughter of a shoemaker, went on the stage after Giacomo's birth and had a considerable success. "A very handsome, shrewd widow," is Goldoni's description of her. As her profession took her to places as far apart as London and Dresden, she was often out of touch with her family, but she seems to have seen to it that they were well looked after in her absences. As late as Giacomo's eighteenth year she was exerting herself in his interests, in a vain attempt to settle him in an ecclesiastical career. But from his eighth year onwards, he was in the charge of his grandmother, the shoemaker's widow, his mother having removed to Dresden, where the Elector of Saxony looked after her interests, attaching her to his Court Theatre for the remainder of her life. One of her daughters joined her there, and her son Giovanni eventually became Director of the Academy of Painting at Dresden. Another of her sons, François, was also a painter, specialising in military subjects, and his work is still to be seen in Paris and Vienna. " Brother of the famous painter of that name " is the title the Prince de Ligne gives to his reminiscences of Casanova.

Havelock Ellis, in his essay on Casanova, says that

all the physical and mental potency of the family was
intensely concentrated in Casanova. This was Casanova's view, too. His references to François and
Giovanni, whom he frequently ran across in his
travels, are kindly but pitying. His younger
brother, he says, ruined himself by two imprudent
marriages; and the elder, though otherwise happily
married, was impotent. His wife, Casanova says,
grieved deeply, for she did not know that her husband was impotent, and fancied that the reason for
his abstinence was that he did not return her love.
The mistake was understandable, Casanova adds,
for his brother was like a Hercules, and indeed was
one, except where it was most to be wished.

Loyalty to his brother prevented Casanova from
alleviating his sister-in-law's distress. All he could
do was to listen sympathetically to the story of how
she had hoped against hope, and, the story over, kiss
her in such a way as to show her that he was not like
his brother.

The son of an actor, and the grandson, through
his mother, of a shoemaker, Casanova was a self-
made aristocrat, conferring on himself an interesting
Spanish pedigree, and assuming the title of Chevalier
de Seingalt. His right to this title was once contested
by an Augsburg magistrate, who accused him of
going about under a false name. Casanova insisted
that he was justified in calling himself the Chevalier
de Seingalt, on the ground that the name was of his
own invention. How can one invent a name, the

magistrate objected. It was the simplest thing in
the world, Casanova explained. The alphabet was
the common property of mankind, and all he had
done was to select eight letters and combine them
in such a way as to produce the word " Seingalt."
But, said the magistrate, a man ought to bear his
father's name. Not at all, said Casanova, for if no
new names had been invented since the creation of
the world every one would be called Adam. Did
not his worship agree ? " I am obliged to," sighed
the magistrate ; " but it's all strange, very strange."

Up till the age of eight and a half, Casanova was
almost an imbecile. Taken by his anxious grandmother to a local sorceress, he returned in the full
possession of his faculties. As a sorcerer himself, he
was inclined, when recording this cure in his old
age, to ridicule the old woman's powers. There
have never been any real sorcerers in the world, he
says, but adds that those who are persuaded by
rascals to take sorcery seriously may perhaps be
influenced by the non-existent forces in which they
believe. " Many things," he writes, anticipating
Dr. Coué, " acquire reality which are first born in
the imagination."

In his teens Casanova was at the University of
Padua, where he took his degree both in civil and
canon law, and obtained his doctorate—achievements which intensive researches among the records
of the University of Padua have hitherto failed to
verify. From Padua he returned to Venice, and

prepared to enter the Church, receiving the tonsure and minor orders from the Patriarch of Venice. Apart from its other advantages, an ecclesiastical career safeguarded Casanova from marriage, a word which, judging from the internal evidence of the Memoirs, he could never hear without a movement of dismay. His first sermon, preached at the age of fifteen, was a triumph, but the triumph was clouded by his passion for a girl, called Angela, who refused her favours unless he gave up the priesthood and married her. Whether it was this unscrupulous suggestion that unnerved him, or whether, according to his own account, he had dined too well, his second sermon ended almost before it had begun. " I delivered the exordium admirably," he writes, ". . . but I had no sooner uttered the first words of the narration than I forgot what I was saying and what I had to say." A swoon, whether feigned or not he is uncertain, delivered him from this impasse. He was carried out of the church, and did not resume his attempt at an ecclesiastical career for another two years.

At what age Casanova lost his pristine virtue, it is impossible to decide. He himself speaks of his double affair with the sisters Nanette and Marton as his first love. The nieces of a pious lady, Madame Orio, at whose house Casanova pursued his suit of Angela, Nanette and Marton sympathised with his unsuccess. He was touched by their affectionate concern, and suggested one evening that as a mark of general goodwill they should all three undress and pass the night in the same bed. Their hesitation offended him ; it showed a lack of confidence in his probity, he said. Besides, he continued, they were two to one. What had they to fear? Convinced by this reasoning, they undressed and joined him in bed, where, failing to present a united front to the enemy, they were engaged singly and overcome.

This affair, which lasted till he left Venice, was, he says, too happy and untroubled to teach him anything about life. " Often, all three of us," he writes, " experienced the need to lift up our souls to eternal Providence in gratitude for the shield it had interposed between us and all those accidents which might have troubled the sweet tranquillity we enjoyed."

At eighteen, his mother having persuaded an old friend, Bernardo de Bernardis, Bishop of Martórano in Calabria, to take Giacomo into his service, Casanova left Venice for Southern Italy. The account he gives of his first voyage into the world is extraordinarily vivid. Nowhere else in the Memoirs does the reader feel more close to the reality of Casanova's life.

The first stage of his journey was from Venice to Ancona, which he accomplished in the retinue of the Venetian ambassador. He left Venice, he says, full of joy and without a single regret. In his purse were fifty sequins,[1] and he felt that the whole

---

[1] A sequin is about nine shillings in English money.

world was at his command. At Chiozza, where the
Venetian ambassador lingered for some days, Casanova fell in with a one-eyed Jacobin monk, Corsini
by name, who, he thought, would put him in the
way of some amusement. But "the miserable
rascal," as Casanova calls him, was less resourceful
than Casanova had hoped, and merely escorted him
to a brothel. To show his mettle, Casanova says, he
paid his addresses to a poor creature whose ugliness
ought to have kept him at a proper distance. After
the brothel, Father Corsini took him to supper with
some friends, and when Casanova returned to his
room, which he shared with the Venetian Ambassador's cook, he had lost all his money at faro.
" Overcome, I lay down near the cook, who woke
up and called me a libertine. 'You are right,' was
all I could reply."

His courage returning the next morning, and a
presentiment of good fortune visiting him, he sold
all his wardrobe, with the exception of three shirts,
a few pairs of stockings, and some handkerchiefs,
searched out his friends of the previous evening, and
returned home penniless again. A few years later,
he says, he revenged himself by writing a diatribe
against presentiments. A presentiment of evil, he
remarks acutely, may be trusted, because it comes
from the mind, but a presentiment of happiness
comes from the heart, and the heart is a fool.

He awoke the next morning, abhorring the light
of day, of which he felt himself unworthy. Not only

had he lost all his money, but, he now discovered, his visit to the brothel had left him with something more concrete than the memory of an ill-spent hour. Weary of existence, he decided to remain in bed and starve to death, but the captain of his ship looking in to tell him he was about to sail, Casanova got up, dressed in haste, tied all his worldly possessions in one of the handkerchiefs he had retained, and went on board.

At Orsara, the next port of call, Casanova went ashore with another monk, a young Franciscan friar called Stephano, who had obtained a free passage from the captain of Casanova's vessel. Stephano took Casanova to a friend of his, an old lady, who supplied an excellent meal of fish cooked in the delicious oil of Orsara, and some exquisite *refosco*. During the meal a priest dropped in, and offered to show Casanova the town. They spent the rest of the day together, and then repaired to the priest's house, where a supper with more *refosco* completed Casanova's reconciliation to existence. The priest himself was tedious, and would insist on reading out his mediocre poems, but his house-keeper was charming, and Casanova passed two nights at the house. In the course of the second night, the housekeeper came to his room, where he made her as happy as circumstances allowed.

On rejoining his ship, Casanova found Friar Stephano laden in every nook and cranny of his holy garments with the alms he had received in

Orsara. These alms included bread, wine, cheese, sausages, preserves, and chocolate, but no money. " Our glorious order," Stephano explained, " does not allow me to touch money, and besides, if I permitted myself to take any while I was begging, my patrons would be quit of me for one or two sous. As it is, I get ten times as much out of them in eatables. Believe me, Saint Francis was a very wise man."

A day or so later the vessel reached Ancona, where Casanova and his companions were quarantined in a lazaretto for twenty-eight days, on the ground that they had come from Venice, and that Venice had recently admitted the crew of two ships from Messina, where the plague was raging. Casanova was much incensed, and affirms in his Memoirs, perhaps inaccurately, that Venice had admitted these crews only after a three-months' quarantine.

Shut up in this lazaretto, with no money, with hardly any wardrobe, and still suffering from his imprudence at Chiozza, Casanova's first taste of the world beyond Venice was not encouraging. But, thirty years later, finding himself in Ancona again, he looked back to this time with tender longing : " It was in this town that I had begun to enjoy life ; and when I reflected that thirty years had passed since then I was overcome ; for thirty years are an immense period in a man's life. . . . What a gulf between the two ages, what changes physical and moral ! I scarcely knew myself. I was as wretched now as I had been happy then ; the fair prospect of a brilliant future no longer shone before me, and, in spite of myself, I had to confess that my time had been unprofitably spent, and my life lived in vain."

Brother Stephano shared Casanova's room in the lazaretto. " A true peasant," Casanova calls him, " who had only become a monk in order to live at ease." But though he disliked the friar, Casanova realised his uses as an expert in the art of being supported by the rest of the world. Stephano could not write, and having ascertained that Casanova could, he dictated to him a number of begging letters, addressed to the superiors of the most opulent convents in Ancona, and to various rich ladies devoted to the cult of Saint Francis. " He made me stuff the letters," Casanova says, " with Latin quotations, even those addressed to ladies, and remonstrance was useless, for he met every objection with a threat to cut off my supplies."

The quantity of wine and provisions conjured out of the recipients of these letters amazed Casanova, who, however, abstained from the wine, in his anxiety to repair the misadventure of Chiozza. One day, after a fortnight of water and careful dieting, he saw in the yard below his balcony a beautiful Greek slave, who had arrived in the retinue of a Turk ; and a day or so later he dropped a sheet of paper folded like a letter from the balcony. It contained nothing, for he was afraid she might ignore it, but as soon as he saw her stoop to pick it up, he dropped a genuine letter, which she picked up, too. It ran :

" Angel of the East, I adore you. I will remain all night on this balcony, longing for you to come, if but for one quarter of an hour, to listen to my voice through the hole beneath my feet. We will speak softly, and in order to hear me you can mount the bale of goods which is beneath the same hole."

The girl followed these directions, which enabled both Casanova and her to listen to each other's voices. During their second conversation, Casanova managed to get the girl half-way through the hole in the plank. " Our pleasures, though barren," he says, " occupied us till the break of day. I put back the plank carefully, and went to my bed in great need of recuperating my forces."

At their third meeting, Casanova dragged her through the hole, and was about to give her the final proof of his affection when the keeper of the lazaretto emerged and seized hold of him. Letting the girl drop, Casanova flung himself on the floor of the balcony, where he lay for some time over-coming an impulse to strangle the keeper.

The next morning he was informed that his quarantine was finished : " As I left with a broken heart, I caught sight of the Greek girl bathed in tears."

After leaving Ancona, Casanova made a pilgrim-age to Our Lady of Loretto, perhaps feeling that he could get a more sympathetic hearing from her than from a saint of his own sex for whatever request he wished to make. Brother Stephano would not accompany him, regarding any homage offered elsewhere as a slur on Saint Francis, but they met again a few days later and went on their way together towards Rome, two servants of God whose outward appearance merits a brief description. Stephano was a burly peasant of thirty, stout and red-haired : Casanova was lean and active, brown-eyed, with a beaked nose and retreating forehead. He describes Crébillon, the French poet, as a man of immense stature, towering by three inches over himself. Crébillon appears to have been about six foot four inches, so Casanova was very tall for an Italian.

Casanova's repugnance to the friar had not abated, and they quarrelled and parted company. Yet a few days later they met again, by the inscrutable workings of Providence, according to Casanova, who, however, admits that the friar was indispensable to him. Providence, fortune, chance, call it what you will, he says, forced him to repose his hopes on that fatal monk. " A strange guardian, indeed ! " he cries, " and the destiny that linked me to him a punishment rather than a blessing ! Nevertheless, his presence was welcome, because I did not doubt that he would extricate me from my difficulties, and whatever the power that had sent him to me, I felt I must submit to it in the assurance

that it was Stephano's destiny to escort me to
Rome."

One afternoon as Casanova and his guardian angel
were slogging along, Stephano said he was tired, and
pointing to a wretched-looking house some way off
the road said they would sleep there the night.
Casanova protested, but vainly, and they entered.
Inside was a decrepit old man, lying on a pallet,
two ugly women, three naked children, a cow and a
dog which barked incessantly. Stephano, though
his garments were as usual weighed down with
eatables, demanded a supper in the name of Saint
Francis.

An ancient hen having been boiled for four hours,
without any mellowing effect on its parched and
sinewy carcass, Casanova lost his patience, and
pulled out the materials of a good meal from the
friar's robes. Supper over, the monk and Casanova
lay down on two piles of straw, but before they
could get off to sleep they found themselves strug-
gling in the embraces of the two women. Casanova,
frightened by the barking of the dog, defended what
virtue he possessed with as little movement as
possible, but the stouter-hearted friar, swearing and
snarling, groped about for his stick, and finding it
struck out vigorously. " Ah, God ! " one of the
women cried, and the friar remarked, " I've settled
her."

" Calm returned to the house," Casanova concludes. " The dog, doubtless insensible, made no

sound ; the old man, probably despatched by the monk, coughed no more ; the children slept ; the women cowered out of our reach ; and we passed the remainder of the night in peace."

On awaking the next morning, Casanova was surprised by the absence of the women. A glance at the old man, who was lying dead with a bruise on his forehead, changed his surprise to alarm. He believed that the women had gone to search for assistance and would return to arrest him and the friar, but a roar of rage from the friar, who had just discovered that his robe had been emptied of its provisions, eased Casanova's mind. He realised that the women had made off with the eatables, and would be as anxious to keep out of his way as he out of theirs. Nevertheless, the dead man (and possibly the dead dog and the dead children, but Casanova throws no light on the fate of the minor neutrals) continued to alarm him, and he insisted that the friar and he should leave immediately. A couple of lifts from friendly waggoners removed them to a safe distance from their late host, and on arriving at Pisignano a devout person gave them a charitable welcome. " I slept soundly," Casanova says, " no longer fearing arrest."

At Spoleti, which they reached early the next day, Brother Stephano had two benefactors. The first gave them an excellent meal at midday, the second an equally excellent supper. In order to please his second host, Brother Stephano abused the first one,

IACOB CASANOVA
1725   1798

" Giacomo Casanova "

alleging that his wine was adulterated. Casanova represents himself as hurt by this ingratitude—" I gave him the lie direct, and called him a rascal." Rising early, he decided to leave his graceless companion, but by the time he had formed this decision Brother Stephano was up and ready to start. " I yielded once more to my destiny," says Casanova.

But Rome was not far off now, and Casanova and his guardian angel came to blows between Soma and Terni, the ostensible cause being Casanova's discovery that the friar had stolen a bag of truffles from a beautiful woman who had entertained them at her inn in Soma. Snatching the bag of truffles from the friar, Casanova knocked him into a ditch, and walked to Terni alone. On reaching Terni, he sent the truffles, he tells us, back to his Soma hostess, and early on the following morning entered Rome.

Though his parting from Brother Stephano had been so brusque, Casanova remembered him almost gratefully when he found himself in Orsara again, nine months later. Much had happened in the interval. He had penetrated into Calabria, interviewed his mother's friend, the Bishop of Martórano, and urged him to quit that miserable city, and, in company with Casanova, make his fortune in the outer world. He had returned to Rome, without the Bishop, but with a letter of introduction to the Cardinal Acquaviva. Profiting by this, and other letters of introduction, he had effected an entrance

c

into Roman society, and though he was so unfortunate as to involve himself, innocently, in a scandal which necessitated his leaving Rome, the cardinal had given him seven hundred sequins as a parting gift, to enable him to visit Constantinople, and a letter of introduction to Osman Bonneval, Pacha of Caramania, a French renegade. From Rome he had returned to Venice for a brief visit, and exchanging his clerical dress for a military uniform had embarked at Venice for Constantinople, with a good supply of jewels and ready cash.

On reaching Orsara, he strolled through the place, experiencing a pleasant sensation as he compared his present state with the wretched state he had been in on his previous visit, thanks to Father Corsini's ideas of amusement. In the intervening months he had bought sufficient experience, as he puts it, to safeguard him for the future from Father Corsinis, swindling gamblers, and venal women. He had, too, become somewhat proficient in "straightforward finesse," a quality which he defines as follows : "Swindling is a crime, but straightforward finesse may be regarded as a kind of prudence. Certainly, it is a quality which borders on knavery ; but one must accept that, and the man who, in a crisis, does not know how to exercise his resourcefulness nobly is a fool." In short, he felt that he had " reached the age in which a man can trust his star, if he has his share of courage and a face formed to predispose persons in his favour.

Beautiful I was not, but I had what beauty does not give—an indefinable something which engaged immediate interest and sympathy."

Reflecting on all these things, he remembered the guardian angel whom destiny had appointed to lead him safely from Orsara to Rome. "What a change since then!" he exclaimed, "in money and position! I felt very sure that in the magnificent uniform I was wearing nobody would recognise the wretched abbé who, but for Friar Stephano, would have become—God knows what!"

CHAPTER TWO

SOME MISHAPS AND A VENETIAN SENATOR

CONSTANTINOPLE, romantic at a distance, bored Casanova when he reached it. Turkey, he says, is a country where weariness of life is more deadly to foreigners than the plague. But he lends some glamour to his stay in Constantinople by representing himself as being taken up by a wise, wealthy, and aged Turk, Yusuf Ali, who was very eager to secure him as a son-in-law. The modern belief in the special wisdom of the East was already current in the eighteenth century ; so Casanova portrays Yusuf as not only wealthy and socially important, but also of a profoundly speculative turn of mind. The highest enjoyment, Yusuf tells him, is of the soul, and independent of the senses : a truth which he illustrates by pointing out that the chief pleasure in smoking derives not from the taste of the tobacco, but from watching the smoke, though he does not explain why indulging the sense of sight should rank as an exercise of the soul. More valuable are his remarks on prohibition in eighteenth century Turkey. " Many of the faithful," he says, " think that they may take wine as a medicine. It is the Grand Turk's physician who has made it fashionable as a medicine, and thereby established his own fortune. He has ingratiated himself completely with his master, who is really always ill, doubtless because he is always drunk."

Marriage with his daughter, Zelmi, Yusuf told

Casanova, would ensure his happiness and greatness :
" My knowledge of you," Yusuf said, " convinces
me that married to Zelmi you will be completely
happy, and I foresee that you will become one of the
pillars of the Ottoman Empire."

But Casanova, " urged forward by an ambition
to become famous among civilised and polite
nations, either in the fine arts or in literature or in
any other honourable profession," shrunk from
assuming the turban. Yusuf received his decision
not to marry Zelmi not only without vexation but,
apparently, with rapture. " He told me that by not
accepting his offer of Zelmi, I had so entirely cap-
tured his esteem that he questioned if his regard for
me could have been stronger, had I become his son."
Loaded with presents by Yusuf, whom the least
captious reader of the Memoirs will at this point
dismiss as either mythical or completely senile,
Casanova left Constantinople for Corfu, where he
offered his services to Monsieur D. R., the com-
mander of the galleasses, and was appointed that
officer's adjutant. On his voyage out to Constantinople, he had spent a month at Corfu, where he
had lost most of his money at the tables. Now,
enriched by the sale of Yusuf's presents, he resolved
to gamble with less reliance on fortune and more on
skill : " I was determined to be a dupe no longer,
but to utilise in my play all those advantages which
a prudent young man can obtain without exposing
his honour to unfavourable criticism."

For a time Casanova enjoyed every kind of success. His talk enchanted every one, he was unostentatiously fortunate at play, and he was gradually supplanting his superior officer, Monsieur D. R., in the good graces of Madame F., the most beautiful woman in Corfu. But they were not yet lovers, their caresses still lacked finality, when one evening Casanova heard himself hailed from a window, and looking up saw the most famous courtesan in Corfu, Melulla. He mounted to her room, " mechanically," and listened to her reproaches for having hitherto ignored her. " She did not in any way deserve to possess me," he says. He yielded, however, and returning to his room passed a sleepless night, racked with remorse at the vile outrage he had inflicted on his love for Madame F. In the course of the next ten days or so, he discovered that his infidelity to Madame F. had been punished by two plagues more concrete than remorse. His one consolation was that, as his relations with Madame F. were still platonic, she had escaped sharing in the ill consequences of his hour with Melulla. Hurrying round to her, he confessed his infidelity and its results, congratulated her on having been saved from disaster by the restraint which he and she had imposed on themselves, and added that had he been the unwitting cause of harm to her, he would have avenged her by suicide. Madame F. paled as he spoke, overcome, he says, by the thought of how near he had been to death.

Two months later he left Corfu for Venice. After his fatal meeting with Melulla, he laments, he lost his health, his money, his credit. Cheerfulness, consideration, wit, everything, even his conversational ability, vanished with his good fortune. People no longer listened when he talked, and even his ascendancy over Madame F. faded away, too, until that lovely woman, almost without realising it, ceased at last to love him.

His only consolation, a consolation which throughout his life invariably visited him after every disaster, was that he had learnt a lesson from which he would know how to profit in the future.

On reaching Venice, Casanova threw off his uniform, and became once more his own master— a sentence which reminds the reader that Casanova had been serving his country as a soldier. Being hard up, he tried to retrieve his fortunes by play, and in less than a week was penniless. An engagement as violinist in a theatre orchestra was the best he could do for himself at the moment, and he reflected sadly that with an education which ought to have ensured him an honourable position in the world, with intelligence, a good fund of literary and scientific knowledge, and possessed of those accidental physical qualities which are such a good passport into society, he yet found himself, at the age of twenty, a poor acolyte of a sublime art, in which, if great talent is rightly admired, mediocrity is as rightly despised.

The orchestra in which Casanova played num-
bered seven members, and when off duty these
young musicians used to roam round Venice making
things uncomfortable for law-abiding citizens. They
would unmoor the gondolas of the patricians,
enjoying by anticipation the curses of the gon-
doliers the next morning. They would rouse up
midwives and send them post-haste to houses where
they were not wanted. Doctors and priests, bearing
the last sacraments, were sent on similar fool's-
errands. They cut the bell-wires in houses, roused
the inhabitants of a parish from sleep by ringing the
church bells, took gondolas across the canal and
ran off without paying, and raided brothels, turning
out the clients they found there, and refusing to
pay the girls after enjoying them.

Two " trivial mishaps," as he calls them, which
compelled him a little later to leave Venice for a
time, complete our idea of the youthful Casanova
on this side of his character.

A grocer called Demetrio, who lived in the same
house as Casanova, a Greek of forty-five to fifty,
having been deprived of his mistress by Casanova,
sawed through a plank above a deep ditch, across
which Casanova used to pass each day. The plank
broke under Casanova, and he found himself up
to the chin in stinking mud. Compelled, in spite
of his inward rage, to treat the matter with " a
factitious levity," so as to be in harmony with his
friends who were laughing on the bank, Casanova

remained in this situation until the arrival of some peasants who dragged him out with considerable difficulty, " et à faire pitié." His dress, a new one, was ruined, and although he continued to laugh he vowed to himself that he would take the most cruel vengeance possible on the perpetrator of this joke.

Having traced it to Demetrio, he went to a cemetery after midnight, cut off the arm of a man buried that day, and entering Demetrio's room the following night pulled his bedclothes off. Demetrio, waking up, was at first amused : " I don't believe in ghosts," he said, " so whoever you are, go away and let me sleep."

Casanova waited a few minutes, and then drew back the bedclothes again. Demetrio sat up and tried to seize his hand, whereupon Casanova held out the corpse's arm. Demetrio pulled at it, Casanova let it go, and Demetrio fell back without saying a word.

The next morning the whole house was in agitation. Demetrio was unconscious and dying, the lodgers said, and abused Casanova, who swore that he knew nothing of what had happened. " At dinner," he says, " I showed myself calm and indifferent. The Greek had been bled, I was told, and could move his eyes, but had not yet recovered the use of his tongue or limbs. On the following day he spoke ; but I learnt after my departure that neither his reason nor the control of his physical faculties had returned to him. The rest of his existence was passed in this melancholy condition. His fate distressed me ; but I consoled myself by reflecting that I had not intended him any harm, and that the trick he played me might easily have cost me my life."

In addition to being cited before the magistrature for profaning the cemetery, Casanova was at the same time cited for rape. In answer to the second charge, Casanova prepared a declaration which he despatched to the magistrate's clerk.

In this declaration he stated that having met a woman and her daughter, aged fifteen, in a tavern, and the daughter having refused his overtures, the mother said : " She is a virgin, and will not give herself without some return." Casanova thereupon paid the mother six sequins, and went off with the daughter, who, however, refused him the privilege he had paid for. At first he was amused, but her resistance presently enraged him ; and, in order to get some value for his money, he administered a beating, the marks of which, he maintained, would still be visible and would support his affirmation that he did not strike her either on the legs or arms. " The mother of this girl," he concluded, " has her six sequins, the girl has preserved her detestable virginity ; and my only crime is to have beaten the infamous pupil of a mother more infamous still."

He was advised, however, by his friend and patron, Signor de Bragadin, not to await trial on either of the charges against him, but " to take the

key of the fields," and absent himself from Venice
for a year or so, till both incidents were forgotten.
He followed this advice, and left Venice by night
for Verona and Milan.

Signor de Bragadin, an important and wealthy
member of the Venetian senate, had some time
previously rescued Casanova from his fiddler's job
in gratitude for the assistance Casanova had given
him in an apoplectic stroke. Casanova happened to
be present when Bragadin was seized with the stroke,
he took the senator home, watched by his bedside,
and on his own initiative removed a mercurial
ointment which the senator's physician had
applied, and which had sent the patient into a
high fever.

"Doctor," said the senator, when the physician
called the next morning, " the person who has
delivered me from your mercury, which was
suffocating me, is a more competent physician than
you."

"I don't know which of us was the more
astonished," adds Casanova, " the doctor, when he
saw an unknown young man, whom he must have
taken for an impostor, pronounced more learned
than himself ; or I, when I saw myself transformed so abruptly into a physician. I remained
modestly silent, though hardly able to contain
my laughter."

The senator, and two of his friends, noblemen like
himself, who had been watching by his bedside,

all agreed that Casanova was gifted with extraordinary powers : " Encouraged by their infatuation, I spoke as a physician, I dogmatised, I quoted authors whom I had never read."

Signor de Bragadin, who had the weakness, Casanova says, to believe in the occult sciences, assured Casanova that he must be supernaturally endowed. " Not wishing to hurt his vanity by telling him that he was mistaken, I confided to him and his two friends, with an extravagant disregard of truth, that I possessed a numerical calculus by means of which I could obtain any information I desired."

Signor de Bragadin said this must be Solomon's key, vulgarly called cabalism. He asked Casanova from whom he had learned that science, and Casanova replied, from an old hermit living on the Carpegna Mountain.

Bragadin and his two friends thereupon put a number of questions to Casanova, who consulted his numerical calculus, and strung together a lot of figures which though meaningless to himself were deciphered by the three old gentlemen in accordance with their own knowledge of the answers. Having survived this test, Casanova was subjected to another. Would he, they asked, teach them the rules of his sublime calculus ? Certainly, Casanova replied. It was true the hermit of the Carpegna Mountain had told him he would die within three days if he communicated the rules to anyone, but he

did not believe the prediction himself. Signor de
Bragadin and his two friends were perturbed. They
were convinced the prediction would be fulfilled,
and from that day never again asked Casanova to
communicate his secret.

It was thus, he says, that he became the hiero-
phant of these three worthy and talented men, who,
in spite of their literary accomplishments, he adds,
were not wise, since they were infatuated with
occult and fabulous sciences, and believed that
through him they possessed the philosopher's stone,
the universal panacea, intercourse with all the
elementary, heavenly, and infernal spirits, and the
power to possess themselves of the secrets of every
government in Europe.

As in the later affair of Madame d'Urfé, and other
similar cases, Casanova feels that his relations with
Bragadin and his friends require some kind of an
explanation. " My dealings with them," he says,
" were not honest in the fullest sense of that term ;
but if the reader to whom I confess myself knows the
world and its standards, I hope he will reflect before
judging me, and perhaps extend me a certain
indulgence." His apology, as always, soon becomes
a justification. Had he tried to cure the three
senators of their delusions, he would not have
succeeded. He would merely have shown himself a
misanthrope, an enemy to the harmless pleasures
of those excellent old gentlemen. It would have
been a failure in common politeness, and, further,

it would have exposed the old gentlemen to exploitation by some unscrupulous rascal.

Signor de Bragadin treated Casanova as an adopted son, giving him, when he was in Venice, an apartment, a servant, a gondola, and a monthly allowance ; and sending him sums of money for many years, to Paris and other places. The whole story, which has a reasonable air of authenticity, reveals Casanova's extraordinary adroitness and audacity, and at the same time goes some way towards explaining why Venice in the eighteenth century no longer ranked among the great powers of Europe.

CHAPTER THREE

HENRIETTE—CASANOVA'S GREAT LOVE

HENRIETTE is the only one of Casanova's loves whose name is familiar to the general reader. He remembers her as the woman for whom Casanova kept a special niche in his congested memory, the woman who loved him till his death and wrote to him in his desolate old age a number of letters which prolonged investigations by devoted Casanovists have not yet managed to unearth. Of recent years, some critics have disputed her reality, holding that she is merely one of the imaginary heroines whom Casanova introduces from time to time to raise the tone of his narrative. One objection to this theory is that Henriette's entrance into Casanova's life, whatever one may think of her exit, is not at all in the romantic key. Another, and conclusive objection, if the interpretation of the Henriette story given in this chapter is the true one, is that Henriette was a very clever adventuress whom Casanova paints romantically, not because he has invented her for the benefit of his readers, but because she invented herself, in her romantic role, for the benefit of Casanova and the furtherance of her own plans.

Casanova met her at Cesana during his exile from Venice after the trivial mishaps already narrated. He had gone to Cesana, in his capacity of sorcerer, on a mission for which he was well paid by his two employers, the Capetani, father and son, whom he characterises as a couple of idiots. The Capetani had heard that a wealthy farmer of Cesana possessed a hidden treasure in his fields, and it was Casanova's task to discover it. The wealthy farmer received him hospitably, and gave him full permission to exercise his magic powers in determining where the treasure lay. Having successfully completed certain preliminary rites, the most important, or at any rate the most minutely described, being a bath privately given by Casanova to the farmer's daughter, Casanova issued forth at midnight on a night of full moon in a sorcerer's robe, a crown on his head, and a wand in his hand, and summoned the gnomes who guarded the treasure to appear. A violent storm broke as he was making his incantations. He was suddenly converted to a belief in his own magic, and cowered within the circle he had traced, devoutly hoping that it would safeguard him against an avenging God, disgusted with his cynical misuse of his powers. The storm passed, and Casanova still lived ; but he was shaken, and having informed the farmer that he had obtained the necessary information from the gnomes, but was not yet empowered to instruct them to raise the treasure, he decided to leave Cesana forthwith.

On the morning of his departure, hearing a great noise in the passage outside his room in the inn where he was staying, he opened his door to find out what was happening. The passage was filled with the police of the local bishop. They had come along, the innkeeper informed Casanova, to ascertain if a person, suspected to be a woman, who was sharing a bedroom with a man, was his wife.

" Enraged by such infamous dealing," Casanova says, " I determined to take a hand in the matter."

The account he gives of his intervention, which included an indignant visit to the local bishop, is rather overcharged. But one may believe him when he says that he was determined to catch a sight of the girl, who had hidden herself under the bed-clothes when Casanova burst in on the gentleman to offer his services.

On returning from his mission, Casanova reported his activities to the gentleman, an elderly Hungarian captain, whose companion was still under the bed-clothes.

" From what country," Casanova asked the captain, " is your travelling companion ? "

" He is a Frenchman, and only speaks French."

The " he " may have been intended by the captain to quench Casanova's interest, and get him out of the room. But Casanova continued : " Then you speak French ? "

" Not a word."

" How amusing ! Then you talk in pantomime ? "

" Precisely."

" I'm sorry for you, it's a difficult language."

" Yes, to express subtleties, but we can make ourselves quite clear to one another in simple matters."

D

" May I ask myself to breakfast with you ? "

" If my friend has no objection."

" Amiable companion of the captain," I said in French, " may I make a third at your breakfast ?"

At these words, Casanova says, he saw coming out of the bed-clothes a fresh, laughing face, with ravishing disordered curls and a man's cap perched on a head which belonged beyond all doubt to a member of that sex without which man would be the most miserable of animals.

His first sight of Henriette decided Casanova to join her and the captain, and travel with them to Parma, which he had previously learnt was their destination. " The beauty of the Frenchwoman had already captivated me. The captain was sixty, if a day, and I naturally thought such a union ill assorted. . . . Vanity apart, I felt myself far better suited to her than her old Hungarian. A charming man, certainly, but he looked his sixty years, while my twenty-three radiated from every glance I gave."

A General Spada, whom Casanova had interested in the affair of the Hungarian captain, invited the captain, his companion, and Casanova to dinner. Henriette dressed as an officer, in a blue uniform, was very entrancing, Casanova says, even in that strange costume. Everyone was delighted with her, except a Madame Querini, who, addressing her in French, said that it was curious she and the captain should live together without ever speaking to each other. "We understand one another excellently," Henriette replied, " for there is very little necessity for speech in our mutual occupation."

Madame Querini affected not to understand the nature of this occupation, and Henriette made it a little plainer by saying that she and the captain played faro, and she held the bank.

" But, tell me," asked General Spada, " does much go into the bank ? "

" The receipts," Henriette replied, " are so small that they are hardly worth mentioning."

Everyone laughed, except the captain, who did not understand French, and might not have laughed even if he had.

Before leaving for Parma with the captain and Henriette, Casanova called on the farmer, and promised to return and bring the treasure to the surface, as soon as certain magical combinations had arranged themselves in a propitious manner. Any attempt by another person, during his absence, to raise the treasure would, he told the farmer, estrange the guardian gnomes, who would immediately sink the treasure to twice its present depth. Therefore, let the farmer keep all impostors at bay. " In this fashion," Casanova adds, " I atoned for all I had done, for, far from deceiving the excellent man, I became his benefactor by safeguarding him against any rascal who might value his money more than his daughter. . . . I trust that the reader will approve this noble termination to my magical enterprise. I don't care to boast, but I certainly think I may congratulate myself upon the way I rounded this matter off."

On the journey to Parma, Casanova learnt that the Hungarian captain had met Henriette a short time previously in Rome, with an elderly officer, whom she had left for the Hungarian, on condition that he would escort her to Parma, where she had some business. He had agreed, and they were now on their way to that city.

This explanation was made in Latin. Henriette confirmed it in French, and asked Casanova to break it to the captain that he and she would have to separate as soon as they reached Parma. "As soon as we reach Parma," she said, "I wish him to let me seek out my own lodging, and make no inquiries at all about me, and, if he should chance to meet me, complete his many kindnesses to me by not giving any sign of recognition."

The captain, though grieved, accepted his fate amiably. But Casanova was both mystified and angry, and as soon as he was alone cried out— "Who is she, this girl who mingles the most exalted feelings with a cynical libertinism. She says that in Parma she wishes to remain unknown, her own mistress, and I cannot, of course, flatter myself that she will not place the same ban on me as on the captain. . . . Good-bye to my hopes, to my money (Casanova had supplied the travelling carriage), and to my illusions ! But who can she be ?

She must either have a lover or husband in Parma, or else respectable parents. Or, maybe, urged on by an unrestrained love of licence, and confident in her charms, she is ready to risk any degradation in the hope of capturing some great nobleman."

His anger rose as his monologue lengthened, and he finally decided to ask her for the same favours she had so easily granted the captain, and, should she refuse, to show her a cold and profound contempt until they reached Parma.

Taking the captain aside the next morning, Casanova asked for permission to propose himself to Henriette as her protector. "The reason," Casanova argued, "why she wishes to sever all relations with you must be that she is expecting to find a lover in Parma. If you will let me have a half-hour alone with her, I flatter myself I can persuade her to sacrifice the lover for me."

The captain was agreeable, Casanova had a private interview with Henriette, she uttered the words "Come to Parma," and Casanova falling at her feet kissed her knees, and swore never to ask for any favour, however slight, until he had shown himself worthy of her precious love. Advised of this happy conclusion, the captain begged to take his leave of Henriette and Casanova, first promising to dine with them on their arrival in Parma. The decision taken by the worthy Hungarian, Casanova says, was agreeable to both Henriette and himself. "Neither of us, it will easily be understood, could be happy until we had dismissed the very recollection of that excellent fellow."

The captain having departed, the lovers sat down to supper, both sad with too great felicity. " Our melancholy was in reality nothing but embarrassment. We loved, yet were still strangers."

Their melancholy and shyness melted after supper. " What a night ! What a woman ! Ah, Henriette, Henriette, how I loved you ! How happy you made me ! "

On arriving in Parma, Casanova took rooms for Henriette and himself, and the best dressmakers of the town soon transformed the impudent young officer into a distinguished and beautiful woman, who, when the Hungarian captain arrived for dinner, called him " my dear father."

" I took my cue from her," Casanova adds, " and called him my friend. My dear wife begged him to dine with us every day.

" Wife," it is worth noting, is Casanova's highest term of endearment. It is sparingly used in the Memoirs, and only where there is no menace of marriage hovering in the background.

The narrative of their stay in Parma, where they spent three months ' in an intoxication of delight,' is a little romanticised in places. There is, for example, a party given in honour of Henriette, attended by the most amiable noblemen of the court. Henriette plays the violoncello with an exquisite art which enraptures everyone. Afterwards Casanova, who had suffered agonies when she began to play, fearing that she would disgrace herself, told her that, having no idea she was a musician, he believed her to have gone mad, and had left the room to weep in privacy over the disaster which had befallen her. To this Henriette replied that it was only a chance remark of his, a month before, about his indifference to music which had kept her silent.

Earlier in the Memoirs, Casanova earns his living as a fiddler, and his fondness for music is referred to more than once. Henriette's triumph at the party required, to give it its full effect, that Casanova should be ignorant of her gift for music. Hence the aversion from music with which he suddenly credited himself. Probably the party, and with it her triumph, are an invention, designed to clothe Henriette in a dignity which should obliterate the memory of her entrance into Casanova's life. On the other hand, the change between the earlier and later Henriette, however much exaggerated by Casanova, was certainly a real if superficial change. Henriette naturally preferred Casanova to the old captain, and in the first stages of the journey to Parma was, one may assume, turning over in her mind both how to transfer herself from the captain to Casanova, and how to erase the first impression Casanova had received of her. The mysterious reasons which made it imperative that she and the captain should part as soon as they reached Parma, and the impressive request that he should not even recognise her if they met, overbore the amiable Hungarian. He had been attracted by her impudent charm, and her officer's uniform. She had joined him without any demur, he had not taken her at all seriously, had paid her ten sequins for her favours, and now that she was converting herself into a woman with a secret, a woman shadowed by some fatality, he was doubtless glad to retire from a situation too complex for an elderly man who wanted only to be amused. What alarmed the captain, fascinated the young and impetuous Casanova. From an easy conquest she had become an elusive enigma ; and as soon as the captain was dismissed, she began to develop her new character for Casanova's benefit. The officer she had been with in Rome was not, she told him, a lover. He was her father-in-law ; and if she had fallen from virtue it was the fault of her husband and her father-in-law, both of whom she characterised as monsters rather than men. Her father-in-law had intended to bury her in a convent. If, to avoid that fate, she had sinned, could Casanova condemn her ? As to those free remarks about the game of faro and the small receipts at the bank, she would never have uttered them, had she been wearing the costume of her sex. These explanations of Henriette took place on various occasions. Her apology for her freedom of speech was made in front of the Hungarian captain, who, in his quality of father, had looked in

for a meal. Casanova was so deeply moved that he
would have flung himself at her feet, to beg forgiveness for not having shown her more respect, but
the captain's presence restrained him. As for the
captain, he sat there petrified with horror at having
treated such a woman as an adventuress. " He
looked at her in great embarrassment," Casanova
says, " and bowed most deferentially, as if in repara-
tion for his past conduct. Henriette, on her side,
seemed to say to him, but without the shadow of a
reproach : ' I am glad you think me worth more
than ten sequins.' "

The mystery in which Henriette involved her
past, and which she refused to dissipate, is not
maintained in a consistent key. At one time she
speaks of her father-in-law as a monster who wishes
to immure her in a convent, at another she says
that she is quite sure that he has never tried to
ascertain where she has gone, after she left him at
Rome. He was only too glad to get rid of her, she
says. Yet her affair with Casanova is terminated
by the arrival in Parma of a mysterious envoy from
her husband or father-in-law, a Monsieur d'Antoine,
who bears her away with him, after a series of interviews, the nature of which she refuses to divulge.
As a final favour, Casanova is allowed to accompany
her and Monsieur d'Antoine to Geneva. " During
our last twenty-four hours," he says, " we were rich
in no other eloquence but that of tears, and sobs,
and those commonplace though poignant reproaches

against the logic of necessity, which happy lovers pour forth when they are forced to part for ever at the height of their happiness. Henriette did not flatter me with any hope to soothe my distress. On the contrary, she said to me : ' Once we are parted by fate, my only friend, never inquire after me, and should you ever chance to meet me, make as if you knew me not.' "

Fortunately, Casanova did not remember that she had used exactly the same words when she dismissed the Hungarian captain. One may reasonably infer that the mysterious Monsieur d'Antoine was acting not in the interests of Henriette's hypothetical husband but on his own behalf. If we assume that Henriette's husband and father-in-law were imaginary beings, the whole story simplifies itself convincingly. First she is with an elderly officer in Rome who bores her, for the Hungarian captain notices that they never talk at meals. She transfers herself to the more genial Hungarian, but he is too old. She is attracted by the young and ardent Casanova, and is happy with him for some months, but no doubt soon realises that he is not a man of solid fortune. She meets Monsieur d'Antoine, assures herself of his wealth, converts him into an envoy from her husband's family, and parts from Casanova, first slipping into his pocket five rolls of one hundred louis d'or each—" feeble consolation for a heart overwhelmed by a cruel separation," Casanova says.

Five hundred louis d'or is a large sum, and confirms the suspicion that Monsieur d'Antoine was a man of means.

The moral of the story is contained in Casanova's own words : " In love, men and women for the most part dupe each other," though one must add that it is difficult to imagine any one duping Henriette.

CHAPTER FOUR

THE TWO NUNS, AND THE ESCAPE FROM THE LEADS

WITH the exception of Henriette, the most famous love of Casanova's life is the nun M. M. Having returned to Venice three years or so after his affair with Henriette, Casanova fell in love with a girl whom he designates as C. C. Her innocence moved him so profoundly that he determined to respect it, and asked for her hand in marriage from her parents, adding that the marriage would take place as soon as he was in a position to keep a wife. For various reasons outside his effective control, he found himself unable to postpone the full expression of his love for C. C., and they entered upon an affair which was interrupted by her father placing her in a convent at Murano. Casanova used to visit the convent church on Sundays, to afford C. C. the pleasure of seeing him, though he could not see her himself. C. C. wrote to him that he had excited the curiosity of all the nuns. " They noticed," Casanova says, " that I neither looked towards the grating, which sheltered the recluses, nor at any of the women entering or leaving the church. The old nuns said that I must be suffering from some great sorrow, from which I had no hope to be delivered except through the favour of the Holy Virgin, and the young ones declared that I was suffering either from melancholia or misanthropy."

Piqued by the mysterious Casanova, M. M., one

of the nuns, and a friend of C. C., wrote to him.
After various misunderstandings, Casanova realised
that M. M. was not trying to hoax him, but really
wished for a meeting. He felt no qualms about
C. C. he says. Rather than be untrue to her, he had
been completely celibate during the previous six
months, and he felt certain that she would recognise
the necessity to his health and spirits of a brief
respite from this exhausting tribute to her charms.

His first assignation with M. M. was in the rooms
of her lover, for she had explained to Casanova that
she was the mistress of a wealthy Frenchman,
Monsieur de B., a very charming gentleman who
had no objection to her using his room to entertain
Casanova. But at this first meeting Casanova had to
content himself with the minor delights of a delicate
and plentiful supper, for M. M. displayed a strange
reluctance to yield to him. Casanova bore this
deprivation with heroic patience, consoled by her
promise to visit him in his own rooms in a few days'
time. To celebrate this occasion he ordered a most
sumptuous supper, and exquisite wines, and graced
his person with the finest slippers he could find, and
a cap in Alençon point.

"I hope my reader will not find me too minute,"
he says. " Let him remember that I was about to
entertain the most accomplished of the sultanas of
the master of the universe." He considered M. M.,
in her quality of nun, as the bride of the Almighty,
and the thought that he was " trespassing upon the

rights of an all-powerful husband " lent the crowning touch to his rapture.

This second meeting answered all his hopes. " I fell into her arms, drunk with love and happiness, and during seven hours I gave her the most positive proofs of my ardour and of the sentiments she inspired in me. . . . At last the fatal bell was heard : our ecstasy had to be cut short : but before leaving my arms she lifted her eyes towards heaven as if to thank her Divine Master for having emboldened her to declare her passion to me."

A few days later M. M. wrote to Casanova, explaining the reason of her reserve during their first meeting, in the rooms of her lover, Monsieur de B. It appeared that Monsieur de B. had secreted himself in a closet, from which he watched his mistress and Casanova, in order to satisfy himself that Casanova was worthy of her. Highly satisfied by his inspection, he now hoped, M. M. went on to say, that Casanova would oblige him by exhibiting his prowess as a lover. " Are you prepared," M. M. wrote, " to let another man observe you while you are indulging the sweet voluptuousness of your senses ? My uncertainty on this point makes me very unhappy, and I beg you to answer—yes or no. Do you understand how my uncertainty troubles me ? "

Surprised at first, Casanova decided on reflection that his part was better than the one accepted by Monsieur de B., and after a hearty laugh resolved to oblige the Frenchman, whom he discovered, a few days later, to be none other than the Abbé de Bernis, the French Ambassador at Venice.

Everything so far had gone to Casanova's satisfaction, but it was now the Abbé's turn. He had heard about C. C. from M.M. , and after some skilful manœuvring placed Casanova in the awkward position of either offering C. C. to him, or showing himself less generous than the Abbé had been about M. M. " Poor young thing ! " Casanova sighed over C. C. " I saw her started on the path of debauchery, and mine was the blame ! " But there was nothing for it except to rival the Abbé's generosity.

A day or two later he heard from C. C., who had dined with the Abbé and M. M. " You cannot imagine," C. C. wrote, " what follies we indulged in after some champagne punch. . . . We spent the night in threes, very agreeable and not too fatiguing. What a charming man ! A man made to be loved ! Though he must recognise himself as your inferior in everything. Rest assured that I shall ever love you, and that you will ever remain the lord of my heart."

A note from M. M. accompanied this letter. " You must feel grateful to me for having completed her education," M. M. wrote, " and for making her altogether worthy of you. I wish you had been concealed in the closet. You would have passed some delightful hours there."

Casanova was much incensed by these two letters,

in spite of C. C.'s tactful " he must recognise himself as your inferior in everything," a sentence which
Casanova may conceivably have added with his own
hand. But being still under the necessity of behav-
ing as gracefully as his French colleague, he
replied in as easy and gallant a strain as he could.
At his next meeting with M. M., he was in low
spirits, which M. M. tried to dissipate by giving him
the fullest particulars of the night she and C. C.
had passed with the Abbé. " I was on thorns,"
Casanova says, " and tried a hundred times to turn
the conversation in a different direction, for the
voluptuous details which she found so pleasing were
most displeasing to me."

The infidelity of C. C., he adds, made him look
at her with different eyes. Marriage with her was
now out of the question, but he resolved that he
would always be her friend.

The story of the nuns dwindles away from this
point, and presently two sisters whom Casanova
loves in succession crowd the Brides of God off
the stage. Whether M. M. and C. C. ever existed
has been questioned, but on the whole the narrative
seems reasonably authentic, if one substitutes someone else for the Abbé de Bernis. The Abbé, who
was the author of one of the most famous treatises
in the eighteenth century, between France and
Austria in 1756, was in Venice in 1753, the year
of Casanova's affair with M. M. ; but numerous
contemporaries, including Casanova himself in a

" Venice in the eighteenth century no longer ranked among the great powers of Europe "

pamphlet written long before the Memoirs, testify to the Abbé's strictness of life during his stay in Venice. It is clear that Casanova borrowed him as his partner in the favours of the two nuns merely to add a little more distinction to the episode. He even makes Bernis leave for Vienna a year earlier than he actually left, in order to represent himself as the Abbé's confidant about the treaty he was manœuvring to bring into existence. " I am going," the Abbé tells Casanova, " to prepare with the Austrian Cabinet a treaty which will be the talk of all Europe." So carried away is Casanova by this picture of himself as the confidant of the famous diplomatist that he does not shrink from heightening the situation by transferring M. M.'s love from himself to the Abbé. " He is gone," M. M. cries to Casanova, " and he confides me to your care. Fatal creature, whom maybe I am condemned to see no more, I thought I loved you but as a friend ! Now that I have lost you, I see my mistake."

Whatever the circumstances which led to Casanova finding himself with M. M. on his hands, she did not remain there too long for his powers of endurance. The affair ended, according to Casanova, by his self-sacrifice in not exposing her to the penalties which would have threatened her as an escaped nun, had he carried her off to Paris, as had been his intention. A similar act of self-sacrifice terminated his affair with C. C., who had written to him that if he would promise to marry her she

E

would refuse all other offers, and await his convenience. He replied that he had no prospects, and that he wished her to be free to avail herself of any advantageous offer which might be made to her.

Nineteen years later he saw C. C. again, and was grieved to find her a widow and poorly off. " If I were in Venice now," he concludes " I should not marry her, for at my age marriage would be ludicrous, but I would most certainly share with her the little I have, and live with her as with a loving sister." As to the Abbé de Bernis, although Casanova has been deprived by modern research of so distinguished a collaborator, he has been given in exchange the Abbé's predecessor at the French Embassy, Monsieur Louis Gabriel de Froulay ; and no one has yet questioned the authenticity of his relations with the English ambassador at Venice, Mr. Murray. These form an interesting pendant to Casanova's connection with the French Ambassador. After Bernis (de Froulay) had left the not quite inconsolable M. M. on Casanova's hands, Casanova struck up an acquaintance with Mr. Murray, " a handsome man, very intelligent, and a great amateur of women, wine, and food. . . . This excellent man soon replaced Monsieur de Bernis (de Froulay) in my friendship, though there was this difference between them that while the Frenchman preferred to watch, the Englishman preferred to be watched." Mr. Murray was in love with a beautiful courtesan,

Ancilla, and Casanova, to oblige his friend, would sit by while Mr. Murray was demonstrating his prowess. Ancilla, however, was in very precarious health, and died the following year. " A quarter of an hour before she rendered up her soul," Casanova records, " her intrepid Briton, yielding to the voluptuous insistency of this modern Messalina, made, in my presence, a last sacrifice on the altar of his love."

All these pleasurable experiences of Casanova's were made possible by the generosity of Senator Bragadin. " His purse was mine," Casanova says ; " he liked my character and my wit." The Senator, according to Casanova, had led a very debauched youth, until an apoplectic fit had pulled him up, leaving him religion and a virtuous life as the only alternative to a sudden death. Seeing in Casanova the image of his unregenerate self, he was filled with pity, and used to pray incessantly to the Almighty to let Casanova see the error of his ways. He would spend many hours delivering moral homilies, to which Casanova listened with pleasure and admiration, while continuing to practise a mode of life which appeared to him open to no really valid objection. " When from time to time," he says, " I surveyed my own conduct, I never failed to esteem it irreproachable, for my excesses made me guilty only in regard to myself. No remorse vexed me. I held that my sole duty was to be an honest man, and this I could pride myself on being."

In a comparatively small town like Venice, the influence which Casanova, a man without birth or position, exercised over an important senator, inevitably aroused envy and suspicion. The Tribunal of the State Inquisition, doubtless after many private representations from persons annoyed by Casanova's love affairs, gamblings, and exaggerated air of self-satisfaction, and alarmed by his reputation as a sorcerer, moved at last, and one day in the month of July 1755, ordered Messer Grande (the title given to the chief of the Archers of the Republic) to arrest Casanova, alive or dead. Casanova was out when Messer Grande came to his house, but hearing of the visit went to Bragadin with the news. " My dear son," exclaimed Bragadin in alarm, " leave at once for Fusina, and from there go as soon as possible to Florence, and stay there till I let you know that you can return without danger."

Conscious of his innocence, Casanova declined to fly. Bragadin began to weep, but, entreated by Casanova to spare him the sight of his tears, pulled himself together, and with a smile of affection embraced Casanova for the last time : " Perhaps, my dear friend, I am fated never to see you any more."

His prediction, Casanova says, was fulfilled. " I never saw him again ; he died eleven years later."

The next morning, July 26, 1755, Messer Grande reappeared, with thirty or forty archers. His first step was to impound Casanova's treatises on magic, which contained formulas for summoning every type of demon. Having thus safeguarded himself against a rescue party from the nether regions, Messer Grande seized the powerless sorcerer, and took him along to the Piombi (The Leads), the prison of the State Inquisition. There he was marched before a man wearing a patrician's robe, who, having surveyed him carefully, remarked : " That is the man. Keep him safe." The gaoler of The Leads thereupon took Casanova over from Messer Grande, and escorted him to his dungeon. No charge was preferred against him, but the report on which the Tribunal acted has been discovered. In this report Casanova is described as a disturber of the peace, a dangerous character who lived by exploiting his friends, notably Senator Bragadin, and as the possessor of forbidden works on magic and necromancy.

Casanova's escape from The Leads, after fifteen months' imprisonment, is the most famous episode in his career. His account of it was written shortly before he began his Memoirs, thirty-two years after his escape. During the long intervening period, he had told the story innumerable times. The escape was, indeed, his chief passport to good society wherever he went, and made him well known throughout Europe. Whether the desire to hear it was as universal and intense as Casanova says is perhaps doubtful ; and after he settled down at Dux the regular inhabitants of the castle must, on

the arrival of a stranger, have exhibited an almost
Casanovan resourcefulness in their efforts to escape
The Escape. So it may have been in deference to
their sufferings that Casanova decided to record
the story on paper. The reason he himself gives
was his desire to relieve himself of the trouble of
telling the story whenever any person of quality, or
personal friend, requested to hear it. It had happened a hundred times, he says, that, after repeating
the tale, he had suffered in health, either in consequence of the sharp remembrance of those melancholy adventures, or from the mere physical fatigue
of narrating all the details. The physical strain
was naturally increasingly severe as old age
approached, and since he would rather, he says, have
succumbed under the strain than laid himself open
to the odious suspicion of disobliging, there was
nothing for it but to put The Escape on paper, and
so at one stroke oblige the rest of the world and
save his own life. He adds that, apart from the
strain, the loss of most of his teeth had impaired the
effect of his spoken narrative. Certain consonants,
forming about a third of the alphabet, cannot be
pronounced without teeth, he explains ; and as he
had doubtless arrived at this truth after many vain
attempts to make himself intelligible, one may be
certain that it was a happy moment for every one
when he took up his pen.

The narrative of his imprisonment and escape,
much condensed, is as follows. His first dungeon

was only five feet and a half high, so he had to stoop when walking to and fro. The heat was excessive, and a neighbouring attic, separated by a grating from his cell, was inhabited by enormous rats, an animal which filled him with horror. Worst of all were the fleas, which disported themselves " in millions " over his body, as he lay sleepless listening to the rats clattering in the attic and to the deafening strokes of the clock of St. Mark's. For some time he had no other distraction than two books brought him by his gaoler, Lorenzo : one of them *The Mystic City*, by Sister Maria de Jesus, of Agrada, the other a plea by a Jesuit for a new Adoration of the Sacred Heart of Our Lord. The Jesuit annoyed Casanova, who calls him " a humbugging rascal, as they all are." But *The Mystic City* amused him, and the ecstatic visions of Sister Maria produced " extravagant dreams " which made him laugh when he awoke. It is a pity he has not recorded any of these dreams. One would have liked a glimpse of Sister Maria's *Mystic City* after Casanova's sleeping fancies had transmuted it into something nearer to his heart's desire.

His confident expectation of being set free almost at once vanished in a few weeks, and he began to set his mind to the problem of escape. Lorenzo permitting him to stretch his legs in the adjoining attic, he searched it for some instrument and found a bolt about a foot and a half long. This he filed on a block of marble into an octangular stiletto, with which he began to dig a hole in the floor of his cell, his intention being to drop into the room below, the office of the Secretary of the Inquisition, and conceal himself under a large table until a chance of escaping unobserved presented itself. In order to prevent Lorenzo from detecting his excavations, he managed to persuade him that it was injurious to his health to have the floor swept, the dust getting into his throat.

Various interruptions, for he was compelled during certain periods to share his cell with others, and the difficulty of the task itself, made the excavation a business of some months. It was finished on the twenty-third of August. Casanova fixed on the twenty-seventh for his escape, but on the twenty-fifth a misfortune befell him, " at which," he says, " I still shudder, though so many years lie between that moment and the present hour." This misfortune was his transference to another cell, which Lorenzo announced with the air of a messenger of good tidings. " You are to be transferred from this cell to another, light and entirely new, with two windows from which you can see half Venice."

Casanova protested, but afraid of raising suspicions yielded quickly, and was led to his new and superior cell. Presently Lorenzo returned in a rage, having discovered the excavation, but Casanova quieted him by threatening to accuse him of having supplied him with tools. " I am a poor man with a family of children," Lorenzo cried, and rushed away clasping his head in his hands.

Casanova soon recovered his spirits, and having got in touch with a fellow-prisoner, Father Balbi, through hiding a letter in a book which Lorenzo, still thick-witted, conveyed to Balbi, Casanova sent the friar his stiletto by an elaborate stratagem, and told the friar to carve his way down into his cell, where he would find Casanova with a complete plan for their joint escape. When, after some weeks' toil, Father Balbi squeezed through the ceiling of Casanova's cell, he was much exasperated to learn that Casanova's plan was of the most nebulous kind, and did not extend beyond getting out on to the very sloping roof of the prison with a rope improvised out of sheets and mattress covers. As for the hole he had bored through Casanova's ceiling its only merit was that it enabled Casanova to climb up into the friar's cell, which was just below the roof. He had in fact been working on Casanova's behalf, and all his reward was the expectation of presently finding himself on the roof of the prison with a companion bent on liberty or death. He yielded to Casanova's insistency however, and helped him to bore a hole through the roof. But the moon was shining brightly, and it was necessary to defer their escape till it had set, after midnight. The intervening hours were spent in talk, chiefly between Casanova and Balbi's fellow-prisoner, an aged Count, whom Casanova begged to furnish the friar and himself with thirty sequins for travelling expenses. The Count pleaded poverty and a large family, and, although Casanova urged his case in a half-hour's speech, the Count, shedding tears of regret at his inability to oblige him, would not contribute more than two sequins, and these only with the proviso that Casanova should return them if, after exploring the roof, he decided to abandon his attempt. Casanova having pocketed the sequins, the Count's scepticism about the chance of a successful escape grew rapidly. On which side, he asked, would they try to get down ? Not on the Piazza side, for there they would be seen by passing citizens. Not by the church, for there they would be shut in by walls. Not by the courtyard, which sentinels constantly patrolled. By the canal side, then ? But they had no gondola, and would have to swim to St. Apollonia, where they would arrive in a miserable condition, and not knowing where to go next.

Father Balbi was impressed, and reproached Casanova bitterly for involving him in such an enterprise. " Alone," Casanova says, " I could not flatter myself that I should succeed. So I mastered myself, and, taking a gentle tone, I told him I was sure of success, though I could not disclose all the details."

The Count's wise advice, he added, would make him proceed with the greater caution. " But I could easily divine," he says, " that what really moved him was the thought of the two sequins which I

should have had to return to him if he had dissuaded
me from my attempt."

The moon had now set, and hanging half the rope
round Father Balbi's neck, and the other half round
his own, Casanova led the way through the opening
in the roof, a moment which he compares to Virgil
and Dante's re-emergence from the infernal regions,
when they saw the stars again.

Crawling up the steep roof, Virgil-Casanova was
much impeded by Dante-Balbi, who clung to the
belt of his breeches. Half-way up Balbi begged him
to stop, for he had dropped a parcel, and believed
it had not fallen further than the gutter. " My first
impulse," says Casanova, " was to give him a kick
and send him to join his bundle ; but, thanks be to
God, I had enough self-control to check this impulse,
for the punishment would have been too severe for
both of us, since alone I could not have accomplished
my escape."

Having reached the ridge of the roof, Casanova
felt more amiable towards his companion, and bid-
ding him rest for a little set off to find some object
to which he could attach the rope. After a long and
agitated search, he discovered a window, through
which he lowered the friar, after repressing an
impulse to stab him with his stiletto, for the friar
had turned irritable again during his vigil on the
roof. Father Balbi was now in a dark room, fifty
feet lower than Casanova, and Casanova's next
problem was how to get down himself, for he could

find nothing to fix the rope to. Another voyage of discovery led him to a ladder, but to get the ladder through the window was extremely difficult, and an awkward movement pushed him backwards over the edge of the roof. For a few seconds he was supported only by his elbows, which rested on the gutter : " It was an awful moment, at which I still shudder, and which it is perhaps impossible to picture in all its horror."

But the thrust which had nearly cost him his life got the ladder into position, and descending it he rejoined the friar. Worn out by his exertions, he dropped on the floor and was immediately asleep. Three and a half hours later, at five in the morning, he was roused by Father Balbi, whose temper was again of the worst. After an hour's hard work they carved their way into one of the offices of the Doge's Palace, escape from which was impossible without gunpowder to blow down the enormous door. " Calm, resigned, and entirely tranquil," Casanova says, " I sat down, and bade the monk do the same. ' My work is accomplished,' I said ; ' It is for God or chance to do the rest. I do not know whether the cleaners will think of coming here to-day, as it is All Saints Day. If anyone comes, I shall rush out the moment the door is opened. You must follow at my heels ; but if no one comes, I stay here. And if I die of hunger, so much the worse.' "

Fresh transports of rage and panic convulsed the friar, who called down every possible malediction on the head of the impassive Casanova. A little later Casanova walked over to the window, where he was perceived by some idlers in the palace courtyard. One of them went to inform the keeper of the palace keys, who, believing he had locked someone in by mistake, hurried up and opened the door. Casanova, followed by the monk, walked out, quickly and with a preoccupied air, and hailing a gondola jumped in, and was rowed off. The fresh air of the early morning, the first sunbeams, and the long canal empty of any gondola but his moved him to tears.

His troubles, however, were not quite over, for he experienced some difficulty in getting off Venetian territory, being compelled on one occasion to extort a loan from a parsimonious friend, a man of sixty, at the point of his stiletto, and on another occasion having to threaten Balbi with premature burial unless he took a different route from himself. But at last he was over the frontier, and making his way to Bolzano took a six days' rest in bed there, while a messenger went to Venice and returned with a hundred sequins from Senator Bragadin.

Balbi had now rejoined Casanova again. "The miserable Balbi," Casanova laments, "gave me every day new reasons for hating his society. He was for ever claiming that without him I could never have escaped, and that by my promise I owed him half my future fortune."

It is difficult to understand why Casanova

troubled himself with Balbi. His own explanation—
" I felt it a matter of conscience to look after the
wretched fellow "—is plainly inadequate. But they
parted company at last, Casanova setting off from
Munich for Paris, and Balbi remaining at Augsburg
with a Canon Bassi, who had interested himself in
the friar through the kind offices of Casanova.

A series of misfortunes and a wretched death are
the almost inevitable consequence, in Casanova's
Memoirs, of seriously annoying Casanova, who,
instead of allowing the reader to picture Balbi living
out his days in peace under the wing of the kindly
Bassi, devotes more than a page to summarising the
later ill-starred career of the friar. Balbi, according
to this report, fled from Augsburg with one of the
Canon's female staff, and a good deal of the Canon's
property. Taking refuge in Switzerland, he tried
to persuade the Calvinists of Chur to adopt him into
their Church, but was speedily thrown out of the
town by that discerning sect. His mistress deserted
him, he returned to Italy, was arrested and taken to
Venice in chains, and immured once more under
The Leads. Nor did freedom, when it came to
him at last, bring happiness. Dissolute and wretched
" he died a Diogenes, but without the intelligence
of that philosopher." On this uncharitable note,
Casanova concludes his narrative of his escape. The
general accuracy of the narrative has been questioned by Casanovan experts, one of whom, Dr.
Guède, tested in his own person the difficulties

which Casanova encountered from climbing on to the roof of The Leads to emerging from the Doge's Palace. The conclusion Dr. Guède came to, possibly while supporting himself by his elbows on the gutter, was that Casanova had found an easier route than the one he claimed to have followed. But whatever the route, it was a great exploit, and one may be certain that Father Balbi's account of it, had he written one, would have testified no less certainly than Casanova's to what the wit and courage of a single man can achieve against almost insuperable odds.

CHAPTER V

REFERRING to his cure as a child by the sorceress to whom his grandmother took him, Casanova remarks that many things become real later which are in their origin imaginary. He was no doubt thinking of the excellent results which sometimes, to his astonishment, followed from his magic cures. On his second visit to Paris, for example, shortly after his escape from The Leads, when he was in his middle thirties, and at the height of his worldly success as one of the directors of the royal lottery, he cured a young nobleman, the Count de la Tour d'Auvergne, of sciatica by cabalism and the application of a lotion which was compounded out of ingredients capriciously selected by Casanova, without any reference to their possible efficacy.

Casanova and the Count shared, with a few others, the favours of an actress called Camille. A girl of fifteen, Babet, whom Camille lent to the Count when she could not visit him herself, attracted Casanova, and one night when he, the Count, and Babet were driving together, Casanova took Babet's hand, and kissed it discreetly in the darkness. She did not withdraw it, and he was becoming more and more ardent, when the Count remarked that he did not feel himself worthy of the courtesies which Casanova, following no doubt the custom of his country, was lavishing on him. These " terrible words," as

Casanova calls them, showed him that he was clasping the wrong hand, and the rest of the drive was as uncomfortable to him as it was pleasant to the Count, who kept on going off into peals of laughter.

This incident, Casanova says, disgusted him with Babet, but attached him with a sincere friendship to the Count, which is Casanova's way of saying that he abandoned the pursuit of Babet on the implied understanding that the Count would not pass the story on to his friends. Their friendship, momentarily clouded by a duel over a loan which the Count was slow in repaying, continued ; and when the Count was confined to bed with sciatica, Casanova undertook to cure him. The preliminaries necessary before the magic lotion could be compounded were somewhat distasteful, and, having in mind Casanova's vindictive temperament, were probably intended to make the Count in his turn feel a fool. Camille, to whom the application of the lotion was committed, was present during these preliminaries, but the Count, so far from being abashed, laughed so much that Casanova had to request him to control himself during the pronouncement of the incantation.

A few days later, Casanova having in the interval forgotten this comedy, as he calls it, the Count called on him to thank him for the astounding efficacy of the cure. " I have an aunt," he continued, " who is well known as an occultist, and for skill in alchemy. She is intelligent, very rich, and sole

F

mistress of her fortune ; and it may do you good to make her acquaintance. She is dying to see you, and insists that she knows you, and that you are not what you seem. She has begged me to take you to dine with her, and I hope you will be so kind as to come. My aunt's name is the Marchioness d'Urfé."

Casanova, realising that his cure of the Count had been due to what he calls " a curious coincidence," was embarrassed by the Count's enthusiasm over his magic powers. He therefore declined to meet Madame d'Urfé at a big reception where his fame as a magician would expose him to invitations from half the aristocratic invalids of Paris, and informed the Count that he would call on Madame d'Urfé in strict privacy only. A dinner was accordingly arranged at which only Casanova, the Count, and Madame d'Urfé were to be present.

Thus began the most remunerative connection Casanova ever enjoyed in his capacity as sorcerer.

" Beautiful, in spite of her age," Casanova writes, " Madame d'Urfé received me with the noble grace of the Court of the Regency. We spent an hour and a half in casual talk, each busy studying the other."

This mutual scrutiny was of more service to Casanova than to Madame d'Urfé, a crazy old lady who had steeped herself in occultism until whatever sense of reality she once possessed had altogether dissolved. The occult sciences were one of the chief occupations of the French aristocracy at this time, with their promise of marvels capable of dispelling

the universal *ennui* ; and money and social position
awaited any one who could impose himself as an
adept in the secret arts, as a master alchemist or
cabalist, as skilled in the migration of souls, or in
correspondence with elementals, or the possessor of
the elixir of youth, or the universal panacea. The
most successful of these magicians, among Casanova's contemporaries, was the Count of Saint
Germain, whom Casanova met several times at
Madame d'Urfé's, and to whom he always refers
with a mixture of respect and vexation. Far cooler
and more self-possessed than Casanova, Saint Germain had a proportionately great triumph. While
Casanova was despoiling Madame d'Urfé, Saint
Germain, who was popularly believed to be three
or four hundred years of age, was taken up by
Madame Pompadour and presented to Louis XV.
The king gave him a suite in the Château of Cham-
bord, where he constructed a laboratory to which
the king would retire when tired of his harem and
immerse himself in chemical experiments, from
which, Saint Germain assured him, the manufactures
of France would greatly benefit.

With such exalted connections, Saint Germain
could afford to leave Madame d'Urfé to Casanova,
who, on his side, affected to be entertained by Saint
Germain's " extravagant boastings," and begged
Madame d'Urfé to ask him frequently to her table.
" Liar and oddity though he was, I cannot say I
disliked him . . . in spite of myself, he amazed me."

Left in peace by Saint Germain, Casanova soon had Madame d'Urfé under his spell. " She firmly believed me," he says, " to be a finished adept, masking my real identity under a pseudonym." Having gained a complete ascendancy over her, he continues, he often abused his power. Looking back, he blushes at his conduct, and exacts from himself the penance of telling the whole truth about how he beguiled her.

" According to her, I possessed not only the philosopher's stone, but also the power of communicating with all the elementary spirits ; from which she inferred, very logically, that I could turn the world upside down if I chose, and be the blessing or the curse of France. The reason I preserved my incognito, she thought, was lest I should be arrested and imprisoned ; which she was convinced would happen if the minister pierced my identity. These extravagances were revealed to her at night by her genius : they were, that is, the dreams of her disturbed mind, which on awaking she mistook for realities. It did not seem to occur to her that, if I were as powerful as she believed, I would be free from the risk of arrest, both because I could foresee it, and because I could overpower whatever force was sent against me. . . . If I had thought it possible to restore Madame d'Urfé to sanity, I think I would have tried to, and it would have been a meritorious task. But I was convinced that her infatuation was past cure, and therefore felt that my wisest line of action was to encourage her in her fantasies and profit by them."

At first, he says, he had no definite plan of profiting by her riches, but contented himself with the agreeable thought that he could do so whenever he wished. She used to tell him that she would give all she possessed to become a man ; and one day, in order to make her drop the subject, he says, though more probably in order to see if there were any limit to her craziness, he told her he could manage the transformation, but it would be necessary to kill her first. She knew that, she said. " All we need," she continued, " is a male child born of an immortal. I am instructed that you will see to this ; and I do not think you will fail in courage from a misplaced pity for this aged body of mine."

At these words, Casanova says, he rose and went to the window, where he stayed for more than a quarter of an hour, reflecting on her infatuation. She scanned his face closely, when he turned towards her again, and said she could see he had been weeping. Picking up his sword and hat, he took leave of her with a melancholy air, drove to the Boulevards in her carriage, and walked there for some hours in profound reflection.

Shortly after this interview, Casanova left Paris for Holland. " I go to Holland for the good of France," he informed Madame d'Urfé, a statement borne out by recent researches in police and diplomatic archives, from which it appears that at

about this time Casanova twice left Paris because
Paris had for the time being had enough of him.
By his own account he was entrusted by the French
government with the conduct of financial transac-
tions which greatly improved French credit, at the
moment in a shaky condition. He also exposed
Saint Germain, who had come to Holland on a
secret mission prejudicial to good relations between
the Dutch and French governments, and forced
" that famous impostor " to flee to England—an
invention which shows how much Casanova's vanity
had suffered from Saint Germain's superior talents.
Nor were his achievements exclusively political,
for he invested some of Madame d'Urfé's money
very profitably on her behalf, and when she begged
him to accept the profit he had made for her he
consented. " She made this offer too delicately
for me to refuse it," he says. No doubt this gift
from Madame d'Urfé, which represented only in
Casanova's imagination the result of his own financial genius, was his chief means of support during his
exile in Holland.

His meeting in Holland with an old love, Thérèse
Imer, whom he was to meet again in London, is
certainly authentic. Thérèse, who was having a
great success as a singer, introduced Casanova to
her two children, a boy of thirteen and a girl, Sophie,
of four or five, whose age and likeness to him,
convinced Casanova that she was his daughter.
Casanova offered to take charge of Sophie, but

Thérèse said she would prefer him to undertake the education of her son.

Casanova, after addressing several remarks to the boy, discovered that he was " insincere and deceitful, always on his guard, watching every word he said, and consequently never saying a word that issued spontaneously from his heart ! "

Thérèse explained that she had trained him in this reserve. " An abominable thing to have done ! " Casanova cried. " You may have strangled in your son all those fine qualities which were his by nature. You have despatched him on the road to be a monster."

Thérèse defended herself by pointing out that she had inspired her son with a horror of lying.

" Excellent ! " Casanova retorted, " but why didn't you go further, and teach him to love truth by displaying it to him in all its radiant beauty. This is the only way to make him lovable, and in this world to be happy one must be loved."

He was leaving The Hague the next day, Casanova concluded, and hoped when he came back to find the boy instructed in a system of morality more consonant with his, Casanova's, views, and more conducive to the boy's happiness.

On his return to Paris, Casanova took the boy with him, and introduced him to Madame d'Urfé as one who might possibly be the instrument of her rebirth as a male. Madame d'Urfé was in ecstasies, and insisted on taking over the boy's education.

A day or two later Madame d'Urfé told Casanova that the boy slept in her bed, " but," she added, " I shall be obliged to deprive myself of this pleasure for the future, unless he promises to behave more discreetly." The old lady was by this time persuaded that the boy, after undergoing an operation unknown to the rest of mankind, would be the means of transforming her into a man. She had given him the name and title of Count d'Aranda, and provided him with tutors of every description. Casanova, after warning her in the interests of her transformation, not to permit the young boy to take any further liberties with her, left her for the time being. His exploitation of the old lady, it has been surmised, was unfavourably viewed in Paris, and he thought it as well to absent himself for a year or so. No doubt he placed Thérèse's son with Madame d'Urfé to act as his representative when he was out of Paris ; and one may infer that his annoyance with the boy's mature prudence, and his warning to the old lady not to encourage the boy's precocity, both derived from a fear that the youthful Count might develop too rapidly, and supplant his chief with Madame d'Urfé. His speech to Thérèse on the loveliness of truth and the beauty of innocence doubtless expresses the retrospective resentment he felt in his old age at the absence of these virtues in Thérèse's son ; an absence which Casanova had some reason to regret both in Paris and in London.

Casanova had now passed his thirty-fifth year, and from this time onward he becomes increasingly restless, impelled ever forward, according to his own account, by his " genius " or familiar spirit, but, according to the researches of his commentators, by the police or by his waning powers of imposing himself on society. At Cologne, for example, he was ejected by the burgomaster, and the account he gives in the Memoirs of his seduction of the burgomaster's wife is clearly unreal even to himself as he pens it in the irritable seclusion of the library at Dux. Exhausted by the vicissitudes of his life, he dreams, one evening in Zurich, of seeking refuge in a monastery : " I shall possess true happiness there," he cries. " Perfect tranquillity." Finding himself the next day in a gorge between two lofty mountains and perceiving a magnificent church to his left, he addresses himself to the abbé, and learns that this is the famous Abbey of Einsiedeln, founded by Jesus Christ in person. But his " genius " baulked his desire for a perfect tranquillity, he took the road again, and after traversing most of Italy returned to Paris once more, where he at once advised Madame d'Urfé of his arrival through his servant Costa : " As he spoke French badly and was rather a fool," Casanova says, " I was certain Madame d'Urfé would take him for an extraordinary being." Madame d'Urfé, crazier than ever, was delighted to see Casanova, and pressed him to set about her transformation into a man. He explained that he must first go to Augsbourg, to confer about the liberation of Querilinto, one of the three chiefs of the Fraternity of the Rosy Cross, from the dungeons of the Inquisition at Lisbon. Until Querilinto was free, nothing could be done. Madame d'Urfé saw the force of this, and promised to send Casanova money and some valuable jewels and presents by his servant Costa.

Casanova set off for Germany ahead of Costa, who had to wait till Madame d'Urfé had got the jewellery and other presents together.

" My fatal genius," Casanova writes of his experiences on this German journey, " had gone *crescendo* from folly to folly ever since I left Turin . . . but I was never so mad as when I went to Munich, where I had nothing to do." The catalogue of his misfortunes was certainly a grim one. Costa, less of a fool than Casanova supposed, went off with the money and jewels entrusted to him by Madame d'Urfé ; a false friend, Desarmoises, introduced Casanova to a woman, the Renaud, who took him to Munich, where " the villainy of the gamesters," renowned all over Europe, deprived him of nearly all his money ; and the Renaud, having engulfed what was left, rejoined Desarmoises, after inflicting on Casanova a malady to which he was by no means a stranger, but which had never visited him so severely before.

He seems to have been entirely subjugated by the Renaud. " This serpent, who crawled out of hell

to destroy me, so subdued me to her will as to
persuade me that she would be dishonoured if I
consulted a doctor during our stay at Munich,
since every one knew that we were living together
as man and wife."

Retiring to Augsburg, Casanova lived on curds,
barley water and manna pills for three months, and
then made up for lost time by a double affair, with
his landlord's daughter and his landlord's cook.
Meanwhile Madame d'Urfé was calling from Paris.
She had furnished a suite of rooms for him in the
Rue du Bacq, she wrote, and was eagerly awaiting
his return. So he went back to " his good angel,"
as he terms her, perhaps with some sincerity with
the memory of the Renaud still fresh in his mind.

CHAPTER VI

THREE weeks were devoted by Casanova and Madame d'Urfé to preparing for her transformation. " Our preparations," he says, " consisted in paying our devotions to the genius of each of the seven planets on the day consecrated to that particular planet. This ritual over, I was to travel, guided by the geniuses, to a place where I would find a virgin, the daughter of an adept, whom I was to impregnate with a male child in a fashion only known to the Fraternity of the Rosy Cross. Madame d'Urfé was to receive the baby into her arms at the moment of his birth, and to keep him beside her in her own bed for seven days. At the end of the seven days she would die with her mouth pressed to the child's, who would thus receive her reasonable soul. . . . As soon as it had reached its third year, Madame d'Urfé would regain her self-consciousness, and I was then to initiate her in the perfect knowledge of the Great Work. . . . And, to begin with, Madame d'Urfé was to make a will leaving everything to the child, whose guardian I was to be till he was thirteen."

Casanova, who preferred to live in comfort at Madame d'Urfé's expense without the trouble of arranging the preliminaries of her transformation, hoped that the old lady would be frightened at the prospect of death. But " the sublime madwoman," looking on her death merely as a detail essential to her resurrection, urged him to set forth at once in quest of the virgin destined to bear the male child who would receive her soul.

In the previous year Casanova had met a pretty dancer, La Corticelli, at Bologna : " a mad young thing," he calls her, " with whom I enjoyed a diversity of pleasures which I shall remember all my life, for she introduced me to a crowd of youthful friends, all of them pretty and complaisant. For a short space of time I lived like a sultan, and the memory of those days is still fresh in my old brain, and I murmur sighing—*Tempi passati !* "

La Corticelli was now in Prague, and Casanova wrote to her to come with her mother to Metz, where he would meet them and escort them to Paris : " To make certain of her coming, I promised her a fortune."

Setting forth for Metz with a well-filled purse Casanova arrived there some weeks before La Corticelli, and whiled away the time with an actress, Raton. " I kept Raton at a louis a day, and she had to be faithful to me, for I never let her out of my sight."

La Corticelli having arrived with her mother, Casanova left Metz for Nancy, where he stayed twelve days instructing La Corticelli in the part she had to play. He had already written to Madame d'Urfé announcing that he was on the way back with a virgin, the last of the family of Lascaris, who had once reigned in Constantinople ; and Madame d'Urfé had replied that she would await them at Pont-Carré, an old castle four leagues distant from Paris, where she would receive the young princess with all possible kindness.

" I am the more bound to her," she concluded, " since the family of Lascaris is allied to the family of d'Urfé, and since I am to be born again in the issue of this happy virgin."

Casanova, anxious to moderate the old lady's erratic enthusiasms, replied, requesting Madame d'Urfé to treat the virgin as a countess, not a princess, and informing her that he would arrive with the countess, and the governess of the countess, on the Monday of Holy Week.

It was, he says, only with immense difficulty that he had persuaded La Corticelli's mother to pass as her governess. " My mother is terribly obstinate," La Corticelli explained, " and with her conventional views always thinks that there's no difference between a governess and a procuress." No doubt Casanova pointed out to the mother that he had both ennobled her daughter and restored her virginity, and that the post of governess to an aristocratic maiden was above suspicion. In any case, the mother yielded, though with a bad grace, and meditating mischief.

The reception of the virgin by Madame d'Urfé at Pont-Carré was very ceremonious. The drawbridge of the castle was lowered, and the old lady stood in the archway surrounded by all her retainers. As soon as La Corticelli had crossed the threshold, she was censed by Madame d'Urfé, receiving this and every other attention with a grave dignity which astonished Casanova.

The consummation of the union between Casanova and the virgin was fixed for the fourteenth of April, when the moon was at its full. Madame d'Urfé herself undressed La Corticelli, scented her, swathed her in a veil, and laid her by the side of Casanova, who performed his part of the ritual satisfactorily. But when Madame d'Urfé asked him the next day if the desired result might be expected at the end of nine months, he replied that he had been informed by his oracle that the operation was a failure because the young Count d'Aranda had watched it from behind a screen. The fatal influence of the young count, Casanova continued, must, according to the oracle, be guarded against if the second operation was to prove successful. He must be sent to some place not less than a hundred leagues from Paris, with a tutor, a servant, and all necessary amenities. Madame d'Urfé, of course, obeyed this command, and the young count, whom Casanova had twice surprised in La Corticelli's bedroom, was despatched to Lyon. La Corticelli and her mother, who had hopes of Count d'Aranda for her daughter, were furious. La Corticelli wanted " her pretty boy " back, she told Casanova, and threatened to make trouble if he were not recalled.

The second operation, the oracle informed Casanova, must take place outside France, under the full moon of May. The place selected by Casanova was Aix-la-Chapelle, and thither he took Madame d'Urfé, La Corticelli and her mother at the beginning of the month. They were well received at Aix, but La Corticelli, who was a ballet-dancer, danced too well at a ball for Casanova's peace of mind. " She attracted every eye," he says, " and I was in tortures, feeling that the opera dancer had been divined beneath the countess. I felt myself dishonoured. Finding an opportunity to speak privately to the young wretch, I begged her to dance like a lady not like a ballet girl ; but she was proud of her success, and had the audacity to tell me that a young lady might dance as well as a professional dancer, and that she was not going to dance to suit my tastes. I was so disgusted with her insolence that I would have got rid of her that instant, had it been feasible. As that was out of the question, I determined that she would not lose by waiting for my revenge. I don't know if it's a vice or not, but I never lose the thirst for vengeance till it's quenched."

The first instalment of his vengeance was not long postponed, for, Madame d'Urfé having given La Corticelli on the day after the ball a casket containing jewellery to the value of sixty thousand francs, Casanova took possession of the casket to prevent her, he says, going off without his leave.

The second operation had been timed to take place at three minutes after four under the full May

"A violent storm broke as he was making his incantations"

moon, but, to the consternation of Madame d'Urfé, La Corticelli writhed and twisted about so violently as to make the fulfilment of the rite impossible. Afterwards, in a private interview with La Corticelli, Casanova learnt that her convulsions would not cease till her casket was restored to her.

Returning to Madame d'Urfé, Casanova inquired of the oracle what was to be done, and learnt that La Corticelli had lost her reason, as a result of having been tainted by an evil genius—an enemy of the Fraternity of the Rosy Cross. Madame d'Urfé accepted this explanation eagerly, and contributed her own view, which was that La Corticelli was with child by a gnome.

A letter to the moon, Selenis, for guidance in their difficulties was the next step decided upon by Casanova and Madame d'Urfé.

The ritual for despatching this letter to Selenis and receiving a reply was complicated. At one in the morning, the hour when the moon was ready to attend to its correspondence, Casanova and Madame d'Urfé undressed, and approaching a bath filled with lukewarm water and perfumes pleasing to Selenis, kindled a libation of spirits of wine in an alabaster cup and burnt the letter addressed to the moon. They then climbed into the bath, Casanova secretly holding in his left hand the moon's reply written in silver characters on green paper. Ten minutes after they had entered the bath, this letter appeared on the surface of the water. Leaving the

G

bath, they dried and scented themselves, and then turned to the letter. "A visible sadness overspread her features," Casanova says, "when she read that her transformation was deferred till the arrival of Querelinto, whom she would see with me at Marseilles in the spring of next year. The genius also said that the Countess Lascaris (La Corticelli) could only do her harm, and that she should follow my advice as to the best method of getting rid of her. The letter ended by ordering her not to leave behind at Aix a certain lady who had lost her husband, and had a daughter who was destined to be of great service to the Fraternity of the Rosy Cross."

The meaning of this last injunction was explained to Madame d'Urfé by Casanova. It referred, he told her, to a Madame and Mademoiselle d'Aché, whose acquaintance he had recently made. The circumstances of his acquaintance with these two ladies he, of course, did not enter into. Attracted by the daughter, Casanova had paid his addresses to her, but her father, a truculent, overbearing person, threatened him with punishment, unless he gave up attempting to seduce his daughter. "Knowing the man to be a brutish, drunken fellow," Casanova says, "who was always ready to draw his sword for a yes or a no, I decided to say nothing and forget the girl, not caring to be mixed up with a man of her father's type." Fortunately, a few days later, Monsieur d'Aché quarrelled with a Swiss officer at billiards. The duel which took place is extraordinarily well described by Casanova, and has an air of complete authenticity. Schmit, the Swiss officer, accompanied by Casanova, went to the rendezvous entirely unconcerned. " Kindly stand at ten paces distance," he said to d'Aché, " and fire first. I shall walk to and fro between these two trees (which were four yards apart)."

D'Aché fired his first pistol without effect. "You have missed me, sir," Schmit said. " I was sure you would. Try again." D'Aché fired a second time, and again missed. It was now Schmit's turn. Firing his first pistol in the air, he covered d'Aché with his second pistol, shot him through the head, and pocketing his pistols walked off.

" I was astounded," Casanova says. " It was like a duel in a dream, or a romance, not like one in real life. I could not understand it. I had not noticed the slightest change on the impassive face of the Swiss."

A second obstacle to Casanova's courtship of Mademoiselle d'Aché still existed, a man called de Pyène, a French officer, who had been d'Aché's second in the duel, and who supported with physical threats Madame d'Aché's demand that Casanova should give her a thousand crowns as compensation for her husband's death By paying a hundred crowns to an officer on the staff of the French commander-in-chief, Casanova managed to get de Pyène transferred to a regiment at some distance

from Aix. " I confess that this was very agreeable
news," Casanova says, on hearing of de Pyène's
removal. " I have never feared to cross swords with
the first comer, though I was never attracted by the
barbarous pleasure of spilling a man's blood ; but
on this particular occasion I felt an extreme repugnance to involving myself with a fellow whom I had
no reason to believe more delicate than his friend
d'Aché."

Nothing now remained for Madame d'Aché
but to bury her hostility to Casanova, which she did
the more readily when he informed her that
Madame d'Urfé was impatient to see her, and would
be delighted if she and her daughter would join
her in her journey to Colmar. " I introduced them
to Madame d'Urfé," Casanova says, " who received
them with a cordiality which greatly surprised
them, for naturally they were unaware that they
had been commended to Madame d'Urfé's care by
the moon." Before the party set off for Colmar,
Madame d'Aché, who felt, Casanova supposed,
that she owed him some return for his kindness,
left him alone with her daughter, a situation by
which he profited to the full.

A truce of sorts had been patched up between
Casanova and La Corticelli, and after Casanova had
parted from Madame d'Urfé for the time being, he
took La Corticelli and her mother to Geneva, gave
her a very beautiful watch as compensation for the
loss of her casket of jewellery, and despatched her

and her mother to Turin. He then rejoined Madame
d'Urfé at Lyon, accepted fifty thousand francs from
her, bade her await further instructions about her
transformation, and departed for Italy in princely
style, where he remained several months.

The last treatment to which he submitted
Madame d'Urfé was at Marseilles, in the spring of
the following year. For Casanova the most important part of the ritual was the throwing into the sea
of a casket filled with lead, which he substituted for a
casket filled with Madame d'Urfé's most valuable
jewels, reserving the original casket for his own use.
The most onerous part of the ritual for him was the
union between himself and Madame d'Urfé, from
which a son was to be born who would be Madame
d'Urfé herself. It was, in fact, only the presence
of a young Venetian girl, whom he had recently
rescued from one of his brothers, which raised his
courage to the sticking point.

"You will be my son," Casanova told Madame
d'Urfé, when the ritual was over, " and when you
grow to be a man I shall not suffer any one to call
you a bastard."

More than one reader, Casanova adds, may say
that it was his business as an honest man to disabuse
the old lady of these baseless expectations. But to
have restored her to reason, he says, even had it
been possible, would only have made her unhappy.
She was really deceived by her own mind ; and
her madness was co-extensive with her existence.

She was doomed to be exploited, and in exploiting her he merely followed the universal law which compels a man to prefer his own interests to that of a stranger.

Satisfied on the whole with his own treatment of Madame d'Urfé, Casanova was disappointed in the various persons he had from time to time associated with himself in his plans respecting Madame d'Urfé. " I cannot refrain," he says, " from the melancholy observation that, with the exception of the young Venetian girl, all my colleagues betrayed me."

The most culpable of them had been La Corticelli, whose miserable end clearly took place only in Casanova's fancy. He met her in Paris, he narrates, on his return from Marseilles. She was abjectly poor, and wasted by a horrible malady.

" Poor Corticelli ! " he exclaimed, " you stir my pity, and in spite of your vile conduct towards me, conduct which has brought you to your present pass, I will not abandon you. See, here are four louis for your most pressing needs, and to-morrow I shall come to you and tell you where to go that you may be cured, and when you are in health again I shall give you your journey money to Bologna. Dry your tears, repent, vow to be good henceforth, and may Heaven take pity upon you."

The wretched girl flung herself on her knees, seized one of his hands, and covering it with kisses and tears, besought his forgiveness. He consoled her, and hastened away heart-broken, to make arrangements for her cure. But his efforts were vain, and within a few days she was dead.

Meanwhile Thérèse had written to Casanova from London, demanding the return of her son, the young d'Aranda. As Madame Cornelis, she was enjoying a great success in London, where she was organising subscription balls and entertainments, to which she managed to give an air of social exclusiveness. She seems to have been a remarkably able woman, a kind of eighteenth century Texas Guinan. Casanova, though annoyed by the insolent tone of her letter, was attracted by the idea of joining her in London. The jewels which he had not cast into the sea at Marseilles had made him rich for the time being, and he was ready for a new adventure. Madame d'Urfé consented to the departure of d'Aranda. The old lady was in an ecstatic frame of mind, and Casanova found it hard to refrain from laughter, he says, as she detailed to him the symptoms of her pregnancy. He adds, however, that when he took his farewell of her, he was moved by a feeling of tenderness he had never hitherto experienced ; a presentiment, he surmises, of their everlasting separation.

A few weeks after his arrival in London, in June 1763, Casanova heard, he says, from a friend in Paris that Madame d'Urfé had died, from an overdose of a liquid she called " The Panacea." She had made a will, leaving everything to the child who should be born of her, and appointing Casanova the governor of the child. "This annoyed me excessively," Casanova says; "for I knew it would make me the laughing-stock of Paris for a week."

All this is invention. Madame d'Urfé did not die till 1775, twelve years later. No doubt Casanova's reason for killing her prematurely was that her family had at last intervened to protect her from further exploitation.

Some years later, during a concert in Paris, Casanova heard someone behind him pronouncing his name with a laugh. Turning round, he saw a tall young man, with two friends. The young man was speaking insolently about Casanova, and said among other things that Casanova had swindled his aunt (Madame d'Urfé) out of at least a million francs.

Casanova rose at once, and exclaiming, "If you were in the street, I'd kick your backside," hastened from the theatre.

CHAPTER VII

LONDON AND LA CHARPILLON

TWO or three weeks before Casanova arrived in London, in the summer of 1763, Boswell met Johnson for the first time, and among other remarks of the Doctor's recorded one, on an unfortunate called Derrick, which might serve as a summary and explanation of all Casanova's wanderings. " Derrick," said Johnson, " may do very well, as long as he can outrun his character ; but the moment his character gets up with him, it is all over."

This year, 1763, Casanova says, marked the turning-point of his life, the beginning of his decline. He was getting short-winded, and was finding it increasingly difficult to keep ahead of his character. For the moment, however, he was very well off, and claims to have had three hundred thousand francs on his arrival in England, obtained from the sale of Madame d'Urfé's jewels.

England pleased him as he drove up from Dover with the young Count d'Aranda. " I noticed first," he says, " the general cleanliness, the beauty of the country, and its cultivation, the goodness of the roads, the reasonable charges for posting, and the speed of the horses, though they never go beyond a trot." On reaching London, he took d'Aranda to his mother, Thérèse Imer, whose name for the time being was Madame Cornelis. Though delighted to recover her son, Madame Cornelis showed no enthusiasm at seeing Casanova again. "She did not give me the caresses I expected," Casanova complains, and continues : "Cornelis told her son that she was working to leave him a fortune at her death, and that she had brought him over because he was now old enough to help her in the running of her enterprise. 'I give twelve balls and twelve suppers to the nobility, and also to the middle classes each year,' she explained. 'I have often five or six hundred guests at two guineas a head. The expenses are enormous, and of course I'm robbed, for I can't be everywhere at the same time. Now that you are here, you can keep your eye on everything, attend to the books, settle the accounts, and supervise the staff during the assemblies.'"

This was gloomy hearing for Casanova, who felt himself far better qualified than the young d'Aranda to look after Madame Cornelis's interests, and had indeed come to England for that very purpose. To add to his chagrin, Thérèse's daughter, Sophie, had clearly been instructed by her mother neither to speak nor to look at him, treatment most wounding to his feelings, since he believed her to be his daughter.

In spite of an impressive experience at a ball given by Madame Cornelis, at which, he says, he met all the nobility of England, and all the Royal Family, excepting the King, the Queen, and the Prince of Wales, Casanova soon perceived that it was a waste of time to visit the ungrateful woman. But like

Father Balbi, La Corticelli, and other persons who had proved unworthy of Casanova's trust, Madame Cornelis was speedily requited for her conduct. Arrested a few weeks later for debt, she sent her son, Sir Joseph Cornelis (formerly Count d'Aranda), to Casanova with a letter in which she begged her kind old friend to procure her release. Casanova replied that he had no time to attend to her troubles, and could only send her his sympathy. Some years later he met Count d'Aranda (formerly Sir Joseph Cornelis) in Italy, and learnt that Madame Cornelis's affairs had gone from bad to worse, and that she was now irrecoverably in debt—" plus que jamais perdue de dettes."

His disappointment over Madame Cornelis did not depress Casanova for long. The English interested him, and though he preferred Paris to live in, and had an ineradicable affection for his native town, he seems to have admired the English more than any other nation. In London, as opposed to Venice, he says, in the account of his arrest by Messer Grande, every one is courageous ; and elsewhere he writes, " England is utterly different from the rest of Europe . . . the most striking feature in the character of these islanders is their national pride ; they rank themselves far above all other nations. ·. . . Everything in England has its own individuality : the fish, the cattle, the horses, the men and the women."

The deference paid in modern London to wealth

and position, and the religious awe which invests
every reference to Royalty, are in strange contrast
with the savagery of the populace as observed by
Casanova, whose remarks on the manners of his
times, though slap-dash, have a certain value. " A
man in court dress," he says, " cannot walk
the streets of London without the risk of being
pelted with mud by the vile mob, while the
gentlemen look on and laugh." Elsewhere he
records that " the Londoners hoot the king, the
queen, and the princes when they appear in public.
They therefore are only seen on great occasions,
when order is kept by hundreds of constables."
He describes, too, an extraordinary riot in Drury
Lane Theatre. Garrick for some reason had presented a different piece from the one which had
been announced. A tumult broke out, the king, the
queen, and the wealthier spectators left as quickly
as possible, and the rest of the audience gutted the
house, leaving nothing but the walls undestroyed.
A fortnight later the theatre was reopened. " When
Garrick appeared before the curtain," Casanova
writes, " to implore the indulgence of the house, a
voice from the pit shouted ' On your knees ! '
A thousand voices repeated the cry, and the English
Roscius was forced to get down on his knees and
beg forgiveness. Then came a thunder of applause,
and everything was over. Such are the English,
and, above all, the Londoners."

Casanova was less impressed by English cooking,

and English Sabbatarianism. "The Englishman is pre-eminently carnivorous," he writes, "he eats hardly any bread, and believes himself economical because he spares himself the expense of soup and dessert, on which I made the comment that an English dinner is like eternity, having neither beginning nor end." As to the observance of the Sabbath, he notes that London abounds in spies, and if they have reason to suppose that there is any gaming or music going on, they slip into the offending house and arrest every one. "But, to balance this," he adds, "the Englishman may with impunity sanctify the Sabbath in the taverns and brothels which exist in such great numbers in London."

Much of the money with which Casanova arrived in England seems to have passed to a number of courtesans without much delay, for he gives us many details of that side of London life. "I visited the bagnios," he says, "where a rich man can sup, bathe and sleep with a fashionable courtesan : a magnificent debauch which costs only six guineas. The expense may be reduced to a hundred francs, but an economy which lessens pleasure has never appealed to me."

Yet he was lonely in the well-appointed house he had rented. "My house seemed expressly intended to contain a mistress in all respectability, and as I had the virtue of constancy, I needed only a mistress to make me happy." After some reflection, he

instructed his housekeeper to put a bill in his window
which ran : " Second or third floor to be let,
furnished, to a young lady who speaks English and
French, and receives no visitors, either by day or
night. Moderate terms."

Having surveyed and rejected a hundred would-
be tenants, Casanova passed as suitable " a girl of
from twenty to twenty-four years, simply but well
dressed ; her face was noble and tender, though
grave ; her complexion a little pale ; her hair
black ; and her beauty without flaw."

The story of Casanova's love for this mysterious
beauty, whose name was Pauline, and who was the
daughter of an unhappy Portuguese nobleman, the
Count of X-mo, clearly belongs, like other romantic
episodes elsewhere in his autobiography, to the
poetry not to the truth of his Memoirs. It was a
relief to the aged memoirist, between the record of
his magnificent debauches in bagnios and the history
of his infamous treatment by La Charpillon, to pen
such sentences as these : " We yielded to a profound
and tranquil slumber. I was the first to awake. A
bright sun lit up the bedchamber, and I devoted
myself to the contemplation of Pauline. As I
gazed at her resting within my arm, this ravishing
woman, the first beauty of Portugal, the only
blossom of a famous family, who had given herself
to me out of love, and who could be mine only
for so brief a space, I heaved involuntarily a deep
sigh. Pauline awoke, and her look, shining and

soft as the first beam of the sun in spring, rested on me in tender trustfulness.

"' Dearest, what are you thinking of?' she asked. 'I am trying,' I answered, ' to persuade myself that my bliss is not a dream. If it be real, I long to die before I lose you. I am that happy mortal to whom you have yielded up an inestimable treasure, but I am not worthy of it, though I love you beyond all words.'"

Marie Anne Geneviève Charpillon, Pauline's successor in Casanova's affections, is as real as Pauline is unsubstantial If nothing were known of her except from Casanova's account, she would still convince one of her reality, but she is also famous as the mistress of John Wilkes, ten years after her meeting with Casanova, and her family history has been reconstructed from police reports, by Monsieur Charles Samaran. The granddaughter of a Swiss woman, Catherine Brunner, La Charpillon was brought up by her grandmother, her mother and two aunts. The grandmother had served her apprenticeship as a procuress in Berne, and had later perfected the art in Paris and London, in association with her three girls. La Charpillon was therefore equipped by training, as well as by temperament and physical gifts, for her vocation, and though only seventeen when Casanova met her she was already an expert in the management of men. ·

"It was towards the end of September 1763," Casanova writes, "that I first met La Charpillon, and from that day I began to die. . . . She was one of those beauties in whom it is difficult to find any positive flaw. Her hair was chestnut coloured, and wonderfully long and thick, her blue eyes were both languishing and brilliant, her skin faintly rosy beneath its dazzling whiteness . . . but the exquisite sensibility one read in her appearance was a lie. This siren had resolved to make me wretched even before she met me, and told me so as if to add to her triumph."

Casanova was taken aback by the impudence with which, at their first meeting, she threatened to make him fall in love with her and then amuse herself by tormenting him. But as he walked away he consoled himself with the thought that the strong impression she had made on him would vanish as soon as he had enjoyed her—" and that pleasure," he murmured, " will not be long delayed."

Calling on her a day or two later, he took, he says, the measure of the company in which he found her, namely, her mother, her two aunts, and three men friends, the Chevalier Goudar, and Messieurs Rostaing and Caumon. He felt, however, that he could look after himself, but the poor dinner provided annoyed him, and his annoyance was increased when La Charpillon invited herself and every one present to supper at his house in three days' time.

Early on the day of " the accursed supper," as he calls it, La Charpillon visited Casanova with one of her aunts, and asked him for a hundred guineas, a sum which would enable her aunt to prepare the Balm of Life. There would be a great sale for it, she said, and Casanova would of course share in the profits.

He replied that he could not give her a definite answer until after supper. The aunt being in another room, he felt that the moment was suitable for her to show her gratitude for his provisional offer, but she eluded his embrace and ran to her aunt laughing. " I followed her," he says, " forcing myself to laugh, too."

When she arrived in the evening, he again tried to embrace her, but without success, and his vexation was not diminished during the meal. " Her hundred extravagances, which would otherwise have enchanted me, only exasperated me, after the two rebuffs I had received from her that day."

He decided not to see her any more. Three weeks later her aunt visited him again : " My niece is a wild young thing," she explained. " She has told me everything. She loves you, but is afraid you are not serious about her. She is in bed now with a bad cold. Come and see her. I am sure you will not leave dissatisfied."

Hastening along with the aunt, Casanova was taken upstairs, and shown into a room where La Charpillon was having a bath. La Charpillon's modesty took alarm, and she cried to him to go away. " My aunt shall pay for this," she exclaimed. Casanova suspected a demand for heavy damages from her male protectors if he touched her. Leaving the room, he went downstairs, and exclaimed, in answer to the aunt's question if he were satisfied—" Yes, I am well satisfied—at having learnt what you are, you and your niece. Here's your reward."

With these words he drew out a bank-note for a hundred pounds and gave it to the aunt. " I lacked the strength to go away without giving her anything, and the procuress was shrewd enough to know it." Casanova resolved to put La Charpillon out of his mind. But when Goudar called on him some days later, he weakened and sent a message to La Charpillon's mother that he would give her a hundred guineas for a night with her daughter. This message brought La Charpillon round to Casanova's rooms in tears. " You have behaved to me as if I were the lowest of prostitutes," she sobbed. " Don't you know I love you ? Do you think it's pleasant for me to be treated like this by you ? . . . Keep your money. I despise it. If you love me, come and conquer me like a reasonable lover, not like a brute, and I will help you, for you can no longer doubt that I love you."

Casanova, deeply touched, willingly agreed to a fortnight's trial of his delicacy, during which time he was not to solicit even a kiss. At the end of the fortnight, which was spent in pleasure parties in London and its environs, and cost Casanova at least four hundred guineas, the night of his reward arrived. The mother, after an unsuccessful attempt

to get a hundred guineas in advance, left the bridal
chamber. Casanova took La Charpillon in his arms,
but she resisted him. Passing from love to frenzy,
he treated her " with the utmost inhumanity," but
could neither overcome her resistance nor draw a
word of protest from her. " Anger, reasoning,
reproaches, threats, tears, atrocious insults "—he
tried each in turn, without success, and at the end of
three hours flung out of the house. The remainder
of the night was passed in sleepless rage. A cup of
chocolate at daybreak proved too much for his
digestion, he was seized with a fever, and returned
to bed, where he remained some days.

After his recovery, Goudar called on him with an
arm-chair, a very elaborate piece of mechanism
which placed any woman who sat on it at the disposal of her lover. But Casanova, while admiring its
ingenuity, shrunk from employing it on his beloved,
with whom he was soon reconciled again. She
expressed her remorse at the way she had treated
him, and agreed to live with him. A house at
Chelsea was rented by the still hopeful Casanova,
he took La Charpillon to it, and they supped
together in the highest spirits. Another night of
resistance ended with a kick from the maddened
Casanova which stretched his love on the floor,
bleeding profusely at the nose.

Reconciled once more, Casanova waited till La
Charpillon had recovered her beauty, which had
been damaged in the scuffle. " I was aching to hold

her in my arms again," he says, " and I bought a magnificent mirror and a fine breakfast service of Dresden china, and sent them to her with a love-letter which must have made her think me either the maddest or the most poor-spirited of men."

Once again Casanova found himself at the beginning of yet another bridal night with La Charpillon. But as soon as he took her in his arms, she burst into tears. " Controlling myself, I asked her whether, if we lay down together, her reluctance would vanish. She sighed, and after a moment's silence answered no. I was paralysed. For a quarter of an hour I sat there without moving, or uttering a word. Then, rising with apparent calmness, I took my cloak and sword, left that hell, and went home to bed."

The final scene of his courtship was played on a tremendous scale. Finding La Charpillon in the embrace of her handsome young hairdresser, he fell upon the barber with his stick. The screams of La Charpillon, half naked behind the sofa, brought her mother and aunts to the rescue. The barber slipped out of Casanova's grasp and vanished. La Charpillon, too, made her escape, and Casanova, to the accompaniment of shrieks from the mother and aunts, vented his unsated rage on the pier-glass, the china and the furniture. At last, exhausted, he flung himself on " the fatal sofa."

But as soon as he realised that La Charpillon was out in the streets, half dressed, in panic-struck flight, he was overwhelmed with remorse. " I was fool enough to express my repentance to the old hags. I begged them to look for her everywhere when dawn appeared, and to let me know of her return that I might run and fall at her feet and beg forgiveness, and never look upon her face again."

He also promised, to the everlasting shame, he says, of his good sense, to pay for all the damage he had done ; and went away, after apologising " to procuresses who made game of me and my honour."

Calling two mornings later, having heard in the interval that La Charpillon had returned, he was not allowed to enter the house. One of the aunts, half opening the front door, informed him that her niece was still delirious, was continually crying out his name in terror, and, according to the doctor, had not twenty-four hours to live. " Fatal barber ! " cried Casanova, and pressing a bank-note for ten guineas into the aunt's hand, went away, filled with terror. The next morning, in a colloquy through the half-open door with La Charpillon's mother, Casanova learnt that the girl was in her last agony. A minister of the Gospel was with her, for medical aid was no longer of any avail—" My poor daughter ! " the mother sobbed. " In another hour she will be no more."

Casanova's knees gave way beneath him as he tottered away. Seeing the gallows before him, he decided to commit suicide, perhaps feeling that to cheat the hangman would close his career on an appropriate note. Buying some balls of lead, he filled his pockets with them and walked heavily down to the Thames, reflecting that only in death could he escape the pale shade of La Charpillon reproaching him as her murderer. At Westminster Bridge he ran into an acquaintance, Sir Edgar ——, a cheerful pleasure-loving young fellow, who, struck by Casanova's solemn expression, cross-questioned him about his errand, and having ascertained it managed, apparently without much difficulty, to persuade him to defer his project.

Two or three weeks later Casanova was arrested and brought before Sir John Fielding, the famous magistrate and half-brother of the novelist. The charge against Casanova was not of murder, but only of intent to do grievous bodily harm to La Charpillon, who was enjoying her usual health.

" I have never given her anything but proofs of my love," Casanova said, in Italian, in which language Sir John Fielding, by whose courtesy and charm Casanova was much struck, had addressed him.

" It is not correct, then, that you wish to do her bodily harm ? " Sir John queried.

" Assuredly not."

" Accept my congratulations. You may dine at home ; but you must find two sureties."

The business of finding two sureties was longer than Casanova had expected. " London is so large ! " he says, by way of explanation ; and while

it was being searched for two persons prepared to
risk money on Casanova's amiability, Casanova was
transported to Newgate. His tailor and wine-
merchant finally offered themselves, Casanova was
brought before Sir John again, and, the sureties
having signed for twenty guineas apiece, and Casanova for forty guineas, he was released. La Charpillon was in court, with her male protectors. " I
was unmoved," Casanova says, " and contented
myself with giving them a look of profound contempt."

As Casanova was leaving the court, five or six
well-known Englishmen arrived, and were much
mortified, it seems, on learning that they were too
late to bail him out.

One would expect to read further on in the Memoirs
of some particularly complex and horrible fate over-
taking La Charpillon, but, possibly because she
was a well-known character, whose history would be
familiar to Casanova's readers, he contents himself
with a very mild vengeance. Before leaving London
he bought a parrot, put it in a cage by his bed, and
repeated to it dozens of times every day the
sentence : " La Charpillon is a bigger whore than
her mother." At the end of a fortnight the parrot
had mastered these words, the effect of which it
enhanced on its own initiative by a shriek of
laughter.

Casanova then put " le perroquet vengeur " up
for sale on the Exchange, where it attracted great

attention. La Charpillon, he says, thought his revenge very ingenious, but the mother and aunts were indignant and consulted several lawyers, who, however, advised them that a bird could not be indicted for slander.

Eventually the parrot was bought by Lord Grosvenor, who presented it to La Charpillon as a mark of his esteem.

CHAPTER VIII

THE LAW'S DESPATCH

CASANOVA left England, in the spring of 1764, in very bad shape indeed. The fortune with which he had arrived was gone, and though his original intention had been to leave London without owing a penny to anyone, for which purpose he had written to Signor Bragadin for two hundred sequins, he actually left London in fear of his life, after taking five hundred and twenty guineas off a broker for a forged bill of exchange. That Casanova knew it was forged does not appear from his narrative, in which he says that the bill was given him by a Baron Stenau, in settlement of a gambling debt, and that he deducted only the amount of the debt, one hundred guineas, and handed the balance to the Baron. The bill, Casanova says, was on a Cadiz business house. It was therefore a week or two before Mr. Leigh, the broker who discounted it, learnt that it was a forgery. He at once wrote to Casanova, requesting the instant return of the five hundred and twenty guineas. " Make haste," the letter concluded, " for this may prove a hanging matter."

Casanova took Mr. Leigh's advice, and made such haste that he was in Calais within forty-eight hours, though delayed at Rochester by convulsions and delirium, due partly to grief at having been the innocent cause of Mr. Leigh losing so much money, partly to the fear of the gallows, and partly to a severe ailment which he had acquired from a mistress of Baron Stenau's. The Baron, agent of so much suffering to Casanova, was, according to the Memoirs, hanged some four months later in Lisbon.

On landing in France Casanova wrote to Signor Bragadin, asking him to forward the two hundred sequins to Brussels instead of to London. Fortunately Signor Bragadin had delayed so long over the original request that this letter reached him in time for him to send the money to Brussels, where Casanova found it a few days later. But for this strange delay on Signor Bragadin's part, the sequins would have reached Casanova before he left London, and he would have been able to meet at any rate some of his obligation to Mr. Leigh. The whole incident (dismissed by Casanova in a single sentence) is thought-provoking, and it is possible that the two hundred sequins were, after all, sent to London, and were used to defray the expenses of Casanova's hurried departure.

Meanwhile Casanova's illness was severe. Passing through Wesel, on the Rhine, he learnt that there was a very capable doctor in the town, and decided to commit himself to this doctor's care. The doctor, urging the need for repose, invited Casanova to lodge in his house. Borne thither in a sedan chair, Casanova dismounted at the door with a handkerchief before his face. " I had not the courage," he says, " to look at the mother and sisters, who were there, with some young girls, when I arrived."

Casanova devotes two poignant pages to his Wesel cure. The boredom of it nearly killed him, he says, and the doctor's cure for the boredom was even more painful, for he sent his sister and two or three of her young girl friends to sew in Casanova's room. In his extreme old age it still hurt him to realise the false impression of his personality which those charming girls had received. " The idea of myself that I left behind me in that house of excellent persons was an absolutely false one. They took me to be the most patient of men ; and the sister and her young companions thought me modesty personified. But these virtues were born of my illness and depression. To judge a man, one must survey his actions when he is healthy and free. Sick and captive, he is not his true self."

From Wesel he went to Brunswick, whither his ill fortune over bills of exchange pursued him. The heir to the throne, a humorous prince, had taken a liking to Casanova, and helped him out of this difficulty ; but rather insensitively, for he handled the impasse which had arisen between Casanova and a Jew money-lender as a practical problem, not as an opportunity for vindicating Casanova's honour.

While this dispute was awaiting its settlement, Casanova retired for eight days to Wolfenbüttel, five leagues from Brunswick, having long been desirous to examine its library, which he speaks of

as the third most important in Europe. The reflections which the memory of these eight days at
Wolfenbüttel arouses in him are very interesting.
As Cromwell, weary of throwing his own Parlia-
ments into the street, cried out that he would
rather be a shepherd watching his flocks than meddle
with the government of men, and as Danton at the
crisis of his fight for life envied the poor fisherman
toiling at his nets, and as Napoleon after Waterloo
congratulated a peasant on his sagacity in not being
Napoleon, so Casanova, bruised by love and money-
lenders, found in the library of Wolfenbüttel the true
home of his spirit.   " I passed eight days there," he
writes, " and never left it except for my lodging,
where I spent only the time necessary for repose
and food. I may count those eight days among the
happiest of my life, since not for one moment during
them was I concerned with my own self. I thought
neither of the past nor of the future. My spirit,
absorbed in work, was conscious only of the present.
Several times since then it has occurred to me that
the true happiness of life resides in moments like
these. I see to-day that a combination of quite
trivial circumstances might have made my existence
in this world as truly wise as it has been truly foolish.
My readers may credit it with difficulty—but I here
proclaim, and thereby condemn nearly all my days,
that virtue has ever charmed me more than vice.
My sins, such as they have been, have only sprung
from lightness of heart. Doubtless many persons

will blame me severely for them. But what
matter ? A man is accountable for his intimate
actions to himself alone, here on earth, and to
God hereafter."

In the last two or three sentences of this medita-
tion one perceives Casanova pulling himself together
according to his invariable habit after he has indulged in any reflections prejudicial to his self-
respect. The form in which he reassures himself is
always the same—a man is accountable only to his
own conscience, and if acquitted there has no cause
for uneasiness. Yet no one had better reason than
Casanova to know that a man is also accountable
to the police, who, judging from the increasing
rapidity with which Casanova passed from one
country to another, were fairly efficiently organised
throughout eighteenth-century Europe. The protection of some important person seems to have
been the only adequate antidote to police officious-
ness, and this protection was hard to come by for
someone as well known as Casanova was at forty,
and still harder to retain. From Frederick the Great,
with whom he secured an interview after leaving
Brunswick, Casanova naturally obtained no favours
of any kind. It would be an exaggeration to say
that Casanova was unaware that Frederick the
Great's faith in human nature was shallower than
Madame d'Urfé's ; but like all men of his type, he
was inexhaustibly optimistic about the likelihood
of other people accepting him at his own valua-

tion ; and when they disappointed him, he was genuinely hurt.

Having, on the advice of Marshal Keith, whom he had met in London, written to Frederick for an interview, Casanova received a note requesting him to be in the garden of Sans-Souci at four o'clock. The king was there to the minute. " Raising his old hat, and addressing me by name," Casanova narrates, " he demanded in a terrifying voice what I wanted. Surprised by this reception, I looked at him without saying a word. ' Well,' he snapped, 'say something. It's you who wrote to me, isn't it ? ' "

Casanova collected his wits, and answered that he had never expected to be so disconcerted by the majesty of a king.

" What do you want ? What do you think of my garden ? " Frederick replied in the same breath.

He thought it superb, Casanova ventured, and the conversation became a little easier. But when the talk arrived at a lottery which Calsabigi, Casanova's partner in the Paris lottery, had recently established in Berlin under Frederick's patronage, Frederick's harshness returned. " It's a pure swindle," the king said, " and I'm not going to have anything more to do with it."

Casanova, who had seen Calsabigi as soon as he reached Berlin, had failed to persuade him to renew their partnership. No doubt, had he been able to interest Frederick still further in the lottery, Casanova would have been in a position to make terms with Calsabigi. But the king's condemnation of the lottery quenched that hope, so he contented himself with endorsing Frederick's opinion of Calsabigi's enterprise. "Your Majesty judges wisely," he said. "It is mere ignorance which deludes people into supporting a gamble of that kind."

Casanova lends a little warmth to the close of his interview with Frederick by representing the king as looking him over from head to foot and complimenting him on his fine appearance. But the interview and still more its sequel disgusted him with Frederick. A few weeks later, he narrates, Frederick offered him through Marshal Keith an appointment as one of five tutors to a new corps of Pomeranian cadets. The offer seemed to him a very good one, and he went along to inspect his future home, the college of the cadets. " Great was my amazement," he writes, " when I saw the abode of these fifteen young gentlemen from rich Pomerania : three or four large almost unfurnished rooms and some whitewashed bedrooms, each containing a wretched bed, a deal table, and two deal chairs. And the cadets themselves, twelve or thirteen years of age, were unwashed, unkempt, and accoutred in a uniform which perfectly matched their rustic faces. Their four tutors were with them. I mistook them for the valets of the boys, and they on their side looked at me in dazed astonishment, not daring to believe that I could be their future colleague."
While he was digesting his disgust, Frederick arrived

on a tour of inspection. " His Majesty saw me,
but did not give me any greeting," Casanova
narrates, and adds : " I was wearing my cross set
with brilliants, and was elegantly dressed."

A necessary article, in a condition unfit for a
monarch to look upon, stood by one of the beds.

" Whose is this bed ? " Frederick cried.

" Mine, sire," said one of the cadets, in a tremb-
ling voice.

" Who is your tutor ? "

The tutor made himself known to Frederick, and
was appropriately dealt with by the savage king.

On returning to Berlin, Casanova called on Marshal Keith, and begged to be excused from accepting
Frederick's offer. He was right to despise such a
post, the Marshal said ; but he ought, nevertheless,
to see the king and thank him before leaving
Berlin. " I confessed my repugnance to another
interview with a man I had found so little sympathetic," Casanova says ; " so the Marshal promised
to convey to His Majesty my thanks and excuses."

Attention to detail, and a taste for inflicting
humiliation, distinguish nearly all great men of
action, and were abnormally developed in Frederick.
One may be fairly certain that the offer of this post
to Casanova, with its uncomfortable sequel, was a
carefully planned amusement, designed to allay
Frederick's annoyance at the self-satisfaction which
he no doubt divined in Casanova during their ramble
round the garden of Sans-Souci.

" Henriette was dressed as an officer in a blue uniform "

From Berlin Casanova set off for St. Petersburg, having first written to Signor Bragadin asking him to remit to St. Petersburg a monthly sum sufficient for his needs.

At Riga he met an old friend, Campioni, and gambled profitably in his company for a couple of months. It was at Riga, too, that he heard of Baron Stenau's death by hanging—"May God rest his soul!" he sighed. He left Riga with some regret, having formed an attachment both to Campioni's wife and stepdaughter. Whether either or both of these attachments passed the limits of mere affection, he does not tell us ; but his little picture of the daughter illustrates his impressionability more vividly than his elaborate descriptive pieces : "Campioni's wife was a charming Englishwoman, rather too thin but bubbling over with wit. She had a daughter of eleven, a very precocious child who looked fifteen, and danced, sang, and played the piano most delightfully. Her eyes threw glances which proved that her development was ahead of her years. I was absolutely captivated by her, and her father complimented her on my conquest, which gave her great pleasure. But her mother hurt her very much by calling her a little baby, a grievous humiliation for a young girl who is beginning to be conscious of her destiny."

The months he passed in St. Petersburg, Casanova says, were not happy. He had plenty of money, but his health, which, he explains, had

I

never been perfect since his escape from the Leads, troubled him a good deal. To make his stay more agreeable, he bought a girl, called Zaire, from her parents. Zaire became too attached to him, her jealousy made her dangerous, and three or four times she tried to prevent him leaving the house. So he had recourse to his stick. " In Russia," he says, " the necessity to thrash is absolute, for words have no force " ; and he illustrates this truth with an episode which reminds one of Gogol, and which shows his descriptive powers at their best. A horse-jobber had driven Zaire and Casanova to Novgorod. On their arrival, Casanova noticed that the horse-jobber was looking melancholy, and on asking the reason was told that one of the horses refused to eat, and was therefore impairing its capacity for work. Casanova accompanied the horse-jobber to the stable, where they found the horse looking sad and listless. " Its master," Casanova continues, " began to address it in a soft and pathetic voice, looking lovingly at it as though to awaken in it a sense of its obligation to sustain its strength with food. The speech concluded, he took the horse's head, kissed it gently, and led the beast into its manger. It was all useless. Then, to my great amusement, he began to weep, with the evident intention of melting the animal's heart. Having wept for some time, he again kissed the horse, and led it again into its manger. But without effect. Maddened by the horse's obduracy, the horse-jobber swore to be avenged, and leading it out of the stable, tied it to a post, took a big stick, and thrashed it for a quarter of an hour. My heart bled for the poor brute. Too exhausted to prolong the thrashing, the horse-jobber led the beast back to its manger, where it set to at once with an excellent appetite, while its master laughed and leapt and committed a thousand extravagances, that the horse might see how happy it had made him."

One of the reasons which cut short Casanova's stay in Russia may have been his fear of losing a member, for he was much affected by the cold, and tells us that he nearly lost one of his ears. True, he consoles himself with the reflection that if he lost a member it might grow again, a scientific fact he had learnt from Prince Charles of Courland, who assured Casanova that his nose had dropped off in Siberia and reappeared the following summer. But he could not be certain, and as there seemed no prospect of a remunerative post about the Court, he decided to leave. Catherine the Great, with whom he conversed two or three times, had hinted at the possibility of finding something for him, but nothing came of it. He speaks of her with affection, however, and lays great emphasis on her modesty, and on her self-control, the exercise of which, he says, required a strength superior to the ordinary emotions of human nature—a sentence in which one may perhaps divine his surprise at the meagre limits within which their relations were confined.

" The demeanour of the great Catherine," he sums up, " at the opposite extreme from that of the Prussian monarch, revealed a genius more vast than his. . . . When one examines the life of Frederick, one admires his courage ; but one realises at the same time that without luck to aid him he must have collapsed. But Catherine owed little to the favours of the blind deity, and succeeded in enterprises which would have startled all Europe had her predecessors performed them, but the splendour of which it seemed her aim to minimise."

From Russia Casanova went to Warsaw, where he fought a duel to which he attached almost as much importance as to his escape from the Leads, and used almost as frequently for the entertainment of others.

Although Casanova seems to have been quite a good swordsman, and records a number of impromptu skirmishes in which he is so consistently victorious as to provoke a suspicion that the skirmishes may have been even more impromptu than he suggests, a formal duel was an experience he was always anxious to avoid. The modern Englishman, whose idea of a duel derives from his reading as a boy of a long line of romantic fiction from Scott to Stanley Weyman, is apt to think that duels were lightly and even eagerly entered upon. But the prospect of death or mutilation was really no more pleasurable to our ancestors than to ourselves. The imperturbability of the Swiss officer facing Monsieur d'Aché's pistol was as extraordinary to Casanova as a similar exhibition of sang-froid in one of our contemporaries would be to us.

When, therefore, Count Branicki, Knight of the White Eagle, Colonel of Uhlans, and friend of the Polish king, accompanied by Lieutenant-Colonel Bininski, walked into the dressing-room of a Warsaw dancer, whom Casanova was congratulating upon her performance in a ballet, one need not be surprised that Casanova cut his congratulations short and prepared to leave the dressing-room. At the best an argument might end in a duel ; at the worst, in so imperfectly civilised a country, in an assassination. But his pacific intentions were baffled.

"It looks as if I have come in at the wrong moment," said Branicki. "Perhaps you are in love with this lady ? "

"I am, my lord. Does not your excellency find her worthy of being loved ? "

"Most worthy ; and, what is more, I am in love with her myself, and am not of a temper to tolerate a rival."

"In that case, I shall cease to love her."

"You give her up, then ? "

"With all my heart, for no one could dispute a lady's favours with you."

"Excellent ; but a man who won't fight for a lady is a coward."

"That's a strong expression ! "

As he uttered these words, Casanova says, he

looked proudly at Branicki, and went out of the
room. Branicki called after him that he was a
Venetian coward, whereupon Casanova returned,
said in calm, firm tones that a Venetian coward
might kill a brave Pole, and without delaying for a
reply left the theatre. He waited outside for
Branicki, sword in hand, but as he waited only a
few minutes his desire to force a fight was baffled,
and he drove away, congratulating himself on the
self-restraint which had kept him from falling upon
Branicki in the dancer's dressing-room.

He hardly troubles to conceal that he was much
depressed by this incident, and that it was only
after sounding the views of the prince-palatin that
he forced himself to send a challenge to Branicki.
But once he had accepted the inevitable he
carried the affair off with a high hand and such a
superfluity of flourish that his less civilised opponent
was thoroughly disconcerted, and got much the
worst of the encounter, being supported half
conscious from the field of honour ; Casanova himself escaping with a wound in his left hand, which
he carried in a sling for at least eighteen months,
thereby no doubt frequently placing himself under
the obligation of satisfying the curious about the
manner in which he came by his injury.

For a short time after the duel, Casanova says, he
was the fashion in Warsaw, went out to dinner and
supper every night, and was compelled to tell the
story of the duel again and again, very often in the

presence of the king. But, suddenly, public opinion turned against him, for no reason at all which he could discover except the notorious fickleness of the Polish temperament. The king, he heard, had been informed that he had been a strolling player in Italy, and that the Parisians had hanged him in effigy for making off with the lottery money. Several challenges were sent to him, which he ignored. He was warned by a friend that his life was in danger, and finally the king sent him an order to leave Warsaw. This order, Casanova was assured, carried no dishonour with it ; and Casanova himself explains it as due to the king's anxiety that he should not be assassinated. Sharing the king's anxiety, he left Warsaw without regret, and travelled to Breslau in Silesia, where he fell in love with a pretty young girl, who like himself was on the way to Dresden. Casanova's mother, and his brother, the painter, were at Dresden, and he was anxious to see them both again.

Maton, as the girl was called, pleased him both by her amiability and by her large appetite, a quality which always charmed Casanova in women ; and on reaching Dresden they settled down in the same apartment. Some of the young officers in the town were attracted by Maton, and one of them, the Count of Bellegarde, pressed his suit with the barest minimum of consideration for Casanova's feelings. " At my age," Casanova, who was now forty-two, says, " I was prepared for disloyalty in a woman ;

yet my vanity had not yet reconciled itself to such a possibility." He took, however, the most careful precautions to safeguard Maton's virtue, and was awaiting a counter-move from Bellegarde with equanimity when a blow struck him from another quarter. The fact that Maton had never left Breslau until her journey to Dresden seems, one does not know why, to have been regarded by Casanova as a guarantee that she was physically in good trim. His indignation was therefore extreme on discovering that his health, never perfect since his escape from the Leads, had been seriously prejudiced by his association with Maton. Separating abruptly from "the infamous Silesian," he retired to his mother's house, and remained there for some time, following a treatment which he had tested with satisfactory results on other occasions. His only comfort in this sad situation was the news, brought him by his brother a week or so later, that the Count of Bellegarde and five or six of his fellow-officers were in the same case as himself.

He was more fortunate at the tables, and having acquired a fair sum by playing with "prudent reserve," he went on holiday to Leipzig, where he met an old acquaintance, the former mistress of the Count of Castelbajac. Her present lover, Schwerin, whom Casanova disliked, was in prison over a forged bill of exchange; so Casanova had little difficulty in persuading her to accompany him to Dresden. She restored his credit as a lover there, he says, for she was not a Maton. Her breeding was good ; her manner modest and dignified ; and after he had baptised her Countess of Blasin, he had no hesitation in presenting her to his mother. One obstacle to their perfect happiness existed. She was suffering from the ailment of which Casanova had just rid himself. A treatment, " mild but carefully followed," soon restored her to health, and they left Dresden for a brief honeymoon, and later travelled together to Vienna.

The Empress Maria-Theresa, a very religious woman, was enthusiastic about chastity, and enforced it in Vienna to the best of her power. On the morning after Casanova's arrival with the Countess of Blasin, two commissioners of chastity entered the bedroom where he and the Countess were taking their morning coffee. Separate rooms at some distance from each other, and the transformation of Madame la Comtesse Blasin into Mademoiselle Blasin, were the results of this visit of inquiry. A few days later Mademoiselle Blasin left Vienna for Montpellier, where her parents lived. " The prodigal child," she said to Casanova, " will find an affectionate father to welcome her back."

At Montpellier she married an apothecary. Casanova, a year or so after they had parted at Vienna, called on her and her husband, and was delighted to find that she was happy with the good fellow, and on excellent terms with her mother-in-law. " I left Montpellier," he says, " with the consciousness that my visit had increased the esteem in which she was held by her husband and mother-in-law ; and I congratulated myself on perceiving that I was capable of a happiness free from any taint of sin." The final touch to the felicity which he experienced whenever he came across an old mistress comfortably settled in marriage was lacking on this occasion. There were no children in the apothecary's home and it was therefore impossible for the apothecary's wife to take Casanova on one side, and ask him in a gentle whisper if he had failed to observe the extraordinary resemblance her eldest child bore to himself.

After Mademoiselle Blasin had left Vienna, Casanova lived quietly for a time, comporting himself respectably, he says. But one evening, while he was dining at home with his friend Campioni, a pretty girl, of twelve or thirteen, walked in on him, made a profound bow, and informed him, in Latin verse, that her mother was waiting outside, and might she come in ? For, unless she were chaperoned by her mother, there would be trouble with the commissioners of chastity. Casanova replying that he had no desire to see her mother, the conversation continued in Latin, developing along lines which made Campioni feel that his presence was no longer necessary. Before leaving, the girl gave Casanova her address.

"On the evening of the next day," Casanova says, " my evil genius inspired me to seek out the lodging of this girl. At forty-two, with my wide experience of life, I was foolish enough to go alone on such an errand."

The young girl admitted him, he went upstairs, and entering a room found himself face to face with a man called Pocchini, an old enemy with whom he had had serious disagreements, in London and elsewhere. Pocchini's wife and a couple of sinister Slavs were also present. Robbed, according to his own account, of his purse, he was also compelled to embrace every one present before he was permitted to leave. " I returned home with death in my heart, and, hardly conscious of what I did, crawled into bed."

The next morning Casanova composed a four-page account of this experience, and was about to call on the police when the police called on him. Led before a high official, the Count of Schrotembach, he was informed that he had twenty-four hours in which to leave Vienna.

" What is the meaning of this unjust and arbitrary order ? " Casanova cried.

" I am under no obligation to explain its meaning," the Count answered. " But I may tell you that you would not have received this order unless you had transgressed the laws of Her Majesty, which forbid games of chance and condemn swindlers to hard labour. Do you recognise this purse and these playing cards ? "

Casanova recognised the purse. It was the one

Pocchini had taken from him. But he was unable to recognise the cards, and, bursting with wrath, handed the Count the narrative of his wrongs which "that hard man" read with frequent bursts of laughter. "We know who you are," said the Count, when his mirth had subsided. "We are perfectly aware why you left Warsaw; and as for this narrative of yours, it's one long string of lies which no one of any intelligence would accept for a moment. You will leave within the time allowed you, and you will inform me whither you propose to go."

"Dear reader," Casanova cries, "it was one of the most terrible moments of my life. I shudder every time I recall it, and it was only a base love of life which restrained me from driving my sword through the heart of that infamous official, a fellow who, in his dealings with me, behaved not like a judge but like a hangman's assistant."

CHAPTER IX

THE DEATH OF A CHRISTIAN

A MANIFESTO against Schrotembach's barbarity was despatched by Casanova to the Empress, to Prince Kaunitz, and to several ministers. Through the kind offices of the Saxon ambassador, who knew Casanova's brother in Dresden, the order of expulsion was suspended for the moment, and this favour, magnified by Casanova's sanguine temperament, seemed to him to portend the arrest and execution of Pocchini and his confederates, and the dismissal of Schrotembach from his post. But its actual significance was trivial ; and a few days later Casanova left Vienna, passionately resolved, he says, to publish the whole infamous story to the world, and to hang Pocchini with his own hands at the first opportunity. " I did neither " he adds.

On arriving at Linz, he wrote a bitter letter to Schrotembach. " I took it to the post in person," he says, " and asked for a receipt, so as to make certain it would reach the scoundrel to whom it was addressed. This letter was essential to the preservation of my health ; for rage kills unless it finds some exit."

Wandering across Germany, Casanova reached Spa, in Belgium, at that time the most famous gambling centre in Europe. There he met an old colleague, Croce, who was accompanied by a beautiful girl of seventeen—" la marquise," Casanova

often calls her, but his habit of ennobling the
women he loved leaves their claims to high birth an
open question. This was the second occasion that
Casanova had come across Croce with a woman more
distinguished than the majority of those he was
accustomed to meet in the company of his fellow-
gamblers. Croce's good fortune disturbed him :
" Without wishing to, I began to wonder about this
man, and his powers of attraction for women of
superior merit. I could not understand it. He
wasn't handsome, he had no culture, no manner in
society, no charm of language. I could see nothing
in him to explain why a girl should leave her
father's house for him."

Casanova attached himself to Croce and la marquise, whose name was Charlotte. Croce's luck at
the tables began to leave him, and some weeks later
he came to Casanova privately, told him he was
ruined, and begged him to look after Charlotte,
who was with child, until her delivery was over.
He himself, he said, proposed to go to Warsaw on
foot, where he hoped to mend his fortunes.

The news of Croce's desertion was conveyed to
Charlotte by Casanova, who assured her that he
would look after her like a father. After she had
recovered from the first shock, she reconciled herself to the situation, and began to care for Casanova.
" She saw that I loved her more than a father," he
says ; " and was grateful to me for respecting her.
Although I held her in my arms for hours on end,

I would only kiss her beautiful eyes, happy in her gratitude and in the joy I derived from my self-restraint. Whenever I felt too strongly tempted, I left her, glorying in my triumph over myself. There was something of the purity of first love in our affection."

From Spa they travelled to Paris. " Throughout the journey my little girl was gentle and sweet to me, and I looked forward to the reward which would be mine after the child was born."

Charlotte's confinement was near at hand, and she was filled with mournful presentiments. Casanova did his best to cheer her, but her presentiments were fulfilled and she died in childbirth, after asking that the baby should be taken to the Foundling Hospital.[1] " An hour before she breathed her last sigh," Casanova writes, " she said good-bye to me in the presence of the venerable ecclesiastic who had confessed her at midnight. ' I know it is good-bye,' she said, and taking my hand raised it to her lips. The tears which fall from my eyes as I write these lines are perhaps the last which I shall consecrate to the memory of that sweet child, victim of a man whose destiny it was to bring wretchedness to those who loved him."

The day before Charlotte's death, Casanova had

[1] Monsieur Charles Samaran has verified the birth and parentage of Charlotte's child from the register of the Foundling Hospital in Paris.

received a letter from his old friend Signor Dandolo in Venice, which he did not open till after the funeral. It contained the news of Signor Bragadin's death. " But I had wept all my tears," Casanova says. " For twenty-two years he had been a father to me, living economically and even going into debt, to supply my needs. He could leave me nothing, for his property was entailed and his furniture and books would go to his creditors. His two friends, Signor Dandolo and Signor Barbaro, who were also mine, were as poor as he, and could give me nothing but their love. With the letter bearing this terrible news was a bill of exchange for a thousand crowns, which, foreseeing his approaching end, Signor Bragadin had sent me twenty-four hours before his death."

A few days later, while Casanova was at lunch, a Chevalier St. Louis called and handed him a document. It was an order from the king to leave Paris within twenty-four hours, and the kingdom within three weeks. No reason was given but that it was " the king's good pleasure," a phrase which excited Casanova's indignation. " An atrocious formula, subversive of human dignity," he calls it.

France was always his favourite country, and his departure from it on this occasion, following so quickly on the deaths of Charlotte and Signor Bragadin, made him keenly conscious of his increasing years, and his precarious future. " I had lost everything," he says. " Death had left me isolated, and I began to be conscious that I had reached what is called ' a certain age ' ; an age which fortune deserts and women despise."

France had been the scene of his greatest triumphs, and as he narrates the story of his enforced departure, the thought of how France, now ravaged by the Revolution, and himself, laid waste by old age, had both fallen from their ancient glory stirred him to an invocation which brings him vividly before us, in his cheerless celibacy at Dux. " Oh, my dear and beautiful France ! " he cries, " where everything went so well in those days, in spite of letters of cachet, and forced levies, and the misery of the people, and the ' good pleasure ' of the king, dear France, what has befallen you ? The people is your sovereign now, the people, most brutal of tyrants. . . . Your government demands abnegation, sobriety, and all the virtues. That cannot last."

Casanova's next objective was Spain. Prudence and cunning are often named together, as though the possessor of one of these qualities is likely to possess the other. This may be so in general, but it certainly was not so with Casanova, who while well endowed in cunning could only survive a strain on his prudence when in the immediate presence of physical danger. Having secured the friendship of the painter Raphael Mengs, who invited him to stay with him in Madrid, Casanova got Mengs into trouble by neglecting those religious observances

K

which, in the country of the Inquisition, were essential to a peaceful existence. Mengs was severely reprimanded for harbouring a heretic, and broke off all relations with Casanova, whose name had been posted on the church door of his parish as an atheist. Not content with this negative proof of his contempt for the Church, Casanova went out of his way to pick a quarrel with a priest who had commissioned a painter to veil the bosom of the Virgin on the altar-piece in his church.

" I came to the point with him at once," Casanova says, " and told him that as an enthusiastic amateur of painting I was deeply grieved at the damage he had inflicted on this superb picture."

" Perish all pictures," cried the priest, " rather than suffer one mortal sin, however small, to be committed ! "

" Let me tell you," Casanova retorted, " that Saint Luke, who, I hope you know, was a painter and portrayed the Mother of our Saviour, using only three colours, would support me in my present protest."

" I can't help about Saint Luke. I have to say Mass at that altar every day, and the picture troubled me."

" Who forced you to look at it ? "

" The devil."

" If your temperament afflicts you like that, you should shrink from no steps, however drastic, to safeguard yourself from temptation. You should have spared the picture, which is a valuable object, not yourself."

"You insult me."

"Do I? It wasn't my intention."

After this barren, though spirited, interchange, it occurred to Casanova that he might have compromised himself with the Inquisition. So he immediately sought out the Grand Inquisitor, whom he represents as a charming man of the world. "It is the priest I blame," said the Grand Inquisitor. "He is clearly unfit to exercise his office. In judging others to be as weak as himself, he has insulted the power of religion. Nevertheless, my dear son, you oughtn't to have annoyed him as you did."

In the course of their chat, the posting of Casanova as an atheist came up. "I would like you to know," said the Grand Inquisitor, "so that you may not leave Spain with wrong ideas about the Inquisition, that the priest who included your name among the excommunicated has been severely reprimanded. It was his duty to see you first, and speak to you as a father."

Secular authority proved less benign than ecclesiastic, and Casanova left Madrid in circumstances which he himself admits to have been the result of his own indiscretion. Further imprudences at Barcelona detained him in the citadel of that town for some weeks; he had already spent some time under lock and key in Madrid; and so was on the whole very glad to get out of Spain, whose castles he had found so much less easy of access than its prisons.

The desire to see Venice once again had been growing in him for some time, but he was still an escaped criminal in the eyes of the Venetian authorities. As a first step to making his peace with them, he composed a refutation of Amelot de la Houssaye's *History of the Venetian Government.* " Having traversed Europe from one end to the other," he says, " the need to look upon my native country once more became so violent that I felt I could not live unless it were satisfied ; and it was therefore less for money than to conciliate the State Inquisition that I composed my refutation." He adds, however, that it was a principle of Venetian policy not to permit any writing, either in attack or defence of the State ; and though he justly says that his position as an outlaw was different from that of the ordinary Venetian, he adduces no convincing reason why the Venetian government, while unwilling to be championed by its law-abiding citizens, should welcome a vindication from the pen of a fugitive from its justice. " After fourteen years of exile," he remarks, summarily, " I was entitled to return to my country ; and I believed that the Inquisitors would welcome the opportunity afforded them by this work of mine to repair the injustice they had done me."

But the Inquisitors let the chance slip by, and for some years Casanova wandered up and down Italy, waiting for a change of heart in the Venetian authorities. As his powers of enjoyment declined, his ambition to make a name for himself in literature, dormant in youth and maturity, asserted itself, and he settled down in Florence to produce, in the intervals of gambling, that perfect translation of Homer's Iliad which Italy still lacked. But one day, to his immense astonishment, a man entered his room, and ordered him, in the name of the Grand Duke, to leave Florence within three days, and Tuscany within eight.

As soon as he had recovered from his stupefaction, he hurried to the magistrate through whom this order had been conveyed to him. Coldly received, he recognised in the magistrate the same person who had banished him from Florence eleven years earlier, through a misunderstanding over a forged bill of exchange. All the satisfaction he could obtain was an assurance from the magistrate that he would, as part of his routine, forward to the Grand Duke any remonstrance which Casanova cared to deposit with him. The magistrate added that the Grand Duke had just left for Pisa, and that there was nothing to prevent Casanova from following him and requesting an audience. But Casanova contented himself with a letter to the Grand Duke. " I write to you, sire," he said, in the course of this letter, " simply to remark that I forgive you, and that, as a consequence of this forgiveness, I shall not expose your injustice, either in writing or by word

of mouth, in the houses of Bologna, whither I go
to-morrow."

An unreciprocated passion in Florence was cured,
he tells us, by this enforced departure : " I spare
my readers the sad details, which I cannot recall
without bitterness. The widow whom I loved, and
to whom I was so weak as to disclose my feelings,
attached me to her chariot wheels only for the
pleasure of humiliating me. She despised me, with
the insolence of youth, and, bent as I was upon
conquering her, I would never have abandoned
the vain attempt had I not been compelled to.
That age, especially when linked to poverty, has
no power over woman's heart was an idea I had not
yet been able to familiarise myself with."

Bologna, where he remained eight months,
pleased him far more than Florence. Its upper and
lower classes were corrupt, but that, he says, meant
nothing to him, for the middle classes were virtuous
and intelligent, and provided him with cultured
talk when he was not at work on the Iliad. The
actresses of the theatre, too, were complacent and
inexpensive, as he learnt through a young·abbé,
called Severini, whom he met shortly after his arrival
in Bologna, and who negotiated Casanova's introduction to various actresses. " Severini was a real
friend," he says, " and kept expenses down . . . but
I must confess that my friendship with him momentarily abated my taste for study, and I laid the Iliad
on one side to await a more convenient season."

Having heard from Signor Dandolo that the Venetian authorities were beginning to relent towards him, and that he ought to settle as near Venetian territory as possible, in order to afford the State Inquisitors an opportunity of realising his improvement in virtue from personal observation, he set off for Trieste. Led, he tells us, a little out of his way by his " genius," or familiar spirit, he broke his journey at Ancona, where he fell in love with Lia, the daughter of his innkeeper, a Jew. Although Lia used to discuss love with him in the most minute detail, his attempts to illustrate some point under discussion with a practical demonstration were always cut short. Unable to sustain any more disappointments, he at last left Ancona for Trieste, but a violent storm drove the boat back into the harbour, he returned to the inn, and Lia yielded to him. This timely storm and Lia's surrender have an air of invention. If this happy ending existed only in Casanova's imagination, the force with which he describes his night with Lia would be explained. Elsewhere Casanova provides no exception to the rule that a faithful report of physical enjoyment informs the reader of what he knows already, but leaves out the particular emotions of the lovers. The surrender of Lia, however, though far from a masterpiece, is faintly touched with an imaginative reality in which someone so unimaginative as Casanova could hardly have invested a real experience of this order.

It was at Ancona that he indulged in those regrets for his youth which we have already given. After contrasting the illusions of infinite happiness which had beckoned him forward then with his present sense of the emptiness and vanity of existence, he continues : " Engaged as I was in trying to get back into my native land, I was forced to recognise that my desires were now limited to retracing my journey through life, to undoing all that I had done, good or ill. Nothing was left to me but to make the inevitable descent to the grave as little irksome as possible. Sombre reflections, these, unknown to youth which laughs when philosophers tell it that beyond the enticing horizon old age is waiting, and misery, and tardy repentance and death."

If, he goes on, these were his reflections at forty-seven, what must his reflections be now at seventy-three, alone in the world, despised, impotent, destitute. " My present thoughts would kill me," he exclaims, " but that I can take refuge from them in my spirit, which, like my heart, remains young. Am I happy or unhappy in the eternal youth of my heart ? Alas, my physical resources can no longer come to the aid of my desires, and what is the advantage of desires which one cannot satisfy ? Nothing is left to me but to kill my *ennui* with my pen. Whether I write nonsense or not, what matter ? I am amused, and I ask nothing else."

He remained two years at Trieste, consumed with

home-sickness. Slavs, Swiss, and Germans are, he remarks, particularly prone to this form of nostalgia, Frenchmen hardly know it, and Italians, with the exception of himself, are almost as immune from it as Frenchmen.

His comparative diffidence as a lover increased during this period. Attracted by a married woman who was still in her teens, he treated her at first with a paternal affection, and then lacked the courage to pass from the father to the lover. " A kind of shame, altogether foreign to my character, hampered me," he says ; and adds that, meeting her four years later, he learnt that she had been perfectly aware of his feelings, and had often laughed to herself at his foolish self-restraint.

For the most part he had to content himself with what he calls " those passing pleasures which last only a quarter of an hour and leave a disagreeable after-flavour " ; but an opportunity once presenting itself of testing whether there is an essential difference between black women and white, he availed himself of it, and decided that there was.

After an absence of some months in Gorizia, where he occupied himself with a History of the Polish Troubles, he returned to Trieste. " I was determined," he says, " to neglect nothing which could secure from the Venetian despotism that favour to which I was entitled after nineteen years of exile, during which I had traversed Europe from one end to the other. . . . It seemed to me reasonable

to suppose that the State Inquisition would find
for me an employment sufficiently well paid to
enable me to live in comfort. I was unmarried, and
required only the necessities of life, for experience
had disabused me for ever of those vain desires
which involve men in disaster."

These are almost the last words in the Memoirs,
which break off just before Casanova's return to
Venice, at the close of 1774. His original intention
was to bring the story of his life down to 1797,
and it has been suggested that he covered at any
rate some of this long period, and that what he wrote
has been lost or destroyed. The history of these
years has, however, been adequately pieced together by the Casanovist scholars, from notes and
correspondence discovered at Dux and elsewhere,
from official archives, and a few other sources.

His return to Venice, when the government at last
granted him his pardon, seems to have been
triumphal. The newly elected Inquisitors were
friendly towards the man whose escape from the
Leads had in the course of time, with some assistance
from his own creative touch, become a picturesque
historical exploit. The chief families, headed by
the Grimianis, took him up and made much of him ;
he set to on the translation of the Iliad with renewed
enthusiasm, and branched out into other literary
enterprises ; and altogether seemed in a fair way to
a secure and reputable existence.

But six years after his return he was earning his

living as a spy on local morals ; and though we have
no details to explain why he was reduced to this
occupation, we may assume, from our knowledge
of his character, that he overplayed his part of the
returned prodigal, clamoured for fatted calves long
after the date for fatted calves was past, and gener-
ally exhausted the goodwill of his benefactors.

The job of furnishing the Venetian Inquisition
with secret reports on everything that was morally
exceptionable in the habits of his fellow-citizens
must have been exquisitely galling to Casanova who
had kept so many spies busy in his prime. In his
resentment he published and distributed all over
Venice a satire on his chief patron, Grimiani ; and
in January 1783, at the age of fifty-eight, found
himself once more beyond the frontiers of his
native country. A few months later, in a fit of
home-sickness, he returned, was rowed through the
canals, and without disembarking looked for the
last time on the scenes from which he had formed
his first impressions of the world.

His wanderings had begun again, and he passed
rapidly through Tyrol, Austria, Germany, Belgium,
Holland, and Paris, where the Revolution was ripen-
ing in a gloomy distracted atmosphere, to Vienna,
and finally to the chance meeting with Count
Waldstein, which provided for his last fourteen
years a shelter from the world in the Castle of Dux,
near Teplitz, in Bohemia.

" The life removed," which the meditative Duke

in *Measure for Measure* preferred to the confused activities of the world, was hateful to Casanova, even in his old age. " The idea of settling anywhere for good was always antipathetic to me," he says. " I could never reconcile myself to the need of adopting a system of prudent conduct." But settled as he was, in spite of himself, he had to reconcile himself to his fate, and so took up his pen, an instrument he never grasped if any more congenial employment was open to him. The history of his Escape from the Leads was the first fruits of his enforced leisure, and was followed by an immense philosophical romance, published in five volumes at Prague, under the title of " Icosameron ou Histoire d'Edouard et d'Elisabeth qui passèrent quatre vingts ans chez les Mégamicres, habitans aborigènes du Protocosme dans l'intérieur de notre globe, traduite de l'anglois." Voltaire, in *Candide*, *Zadig*, and other brief and witty works, had made this combination of story and moralising popular. But Casanova was not Voltaire, although in his long and clearly almost entirely apocryphal account of his talks with Voltaire he represents himself as reducing Voltaire to tears of mingled shame and rapture over Ariosto, whom, until Casanova opened his eyes, Voltaire had hideously misjudged. The adventures of Edouard and Elisabeth among the aborigines of Protocosme interested no one, and Casanova turned his attention to the story of his own life.

" I write away at it for ten hours each day," he

says, " to stifle the black misery which envelopes
my wretched existence, and threatens my very
reason."

His host, Count Waldstein, seems to have treated
him with consideration, though not quite as an
equal ; and Count Waldstein's uncle, the Prince de
Ligne, portrays him at length in his Memoirs, in a
friendly though not uncritical spirit. " Casanova,"
he writes, " his money exhausted, his travels and
adventures over, accepted my nephew's invitation
to take charge of the library at Dux, where, during
six summers, he delighted me with his interesting
and animated talk." The Prince adds, however,
that Casanova was always taking offence at some
fancied slight, either from the Count, or from one
of the staff. " You're a pack of Jacobins ! " he
used to exclaim, adding, when his temper had
expended itself—" I am proud, because that is all
that is left to me."

In addition to these reminiscences of Casanova,
the Prince de Ligne drew his portrait under the
name of Adventuros. " Adventuros," he writes,
" would be handsome, if he were not ugly. He is a
huge man, a real Hercules, and very dark com-
plexioned. His eyes sparkle with life, but betray a
constant irritability, restlessness, and quickness to
take offence. He laughs little, but makes others
laugh ; and knows everything except those things
he especially prides himself on knowing—dancing,
French, good breeding, and knowledge of the world.

He is witty, except in his comedies, and a philosopher, except in his philosophical treatises. But his prodigious fancy, his native vivacity, his travels, the varied parts he has played in life, and the courage with which he sustains an old age barren of riches and pleasure, make him a man well worth knowing, a man deserving even of respect, and of the friendship of those few persons who find favour in his eyes."

The subterranean life of the Castle of Dux would naturally not come within the Prince de Ligne's range of observation, and he therefore assumed that the slights which Casanova saw everywhere did not exist, except in his own irritable fancy. But Casanova was only a superior member of the castle's staff, he was not the guest he appeared to be in his talks with the prince. The other members of the domestic staff were bound to be jealous of him, and Casanova, never even in his most flourishing times tactful and conciliatory, was certain in his savage old age to make things as difficult as possible for himself.

More than twenty letters, some of considerable length, written by Casanova to the steward of the castle, Herr Faulkircher (or Feltkirchner), whom he suspected of causing his portrait to be nailed to the privy door, were found among Casanova's papers. Faulkircher's answers are missing, and it seems probable that Casanova wrote these letters only to relieve his rage, and never sent them to his enemy.

The phrase which Swift used of himself, exiled in Dublin, recurs to one as one reads poor Casanova's screams of fury—" I shall die like a rat in a poisoned hole."

" You know nothing," he writes to Faulkircher, " you have never acquired any of that knowledge which amplifies a man's intelligence, you have never formed yourself by intercourse with men of education, you have never ennobled your spirit with great literature, or shaped your character by the laws of honour and the conventions of social decency.

" All that you lack, I possess. My birth was humble, but I may thank destiny and my good fortune that I have acquired all these distinctions, which raise me so high above you, above you who, a soldier at the age when I was learning to read, have made so remarkable a use of your talents as to rise, in fifty years, to the respectable rank of a sub-lieutenant. . . .

" It is now five years since you came to Dux, and began to puzzle your head why Count Waldstein should throw away a thousand florins a year on a librarian. In your zeal for his interests, you tried to persuade him to get rid of me, and having failed in this aim you set yourself to make my existence here so intolerable that I would abandon it of my own free will. . . .

" And now a word about your friendship with that young blackguard, Viderol. His history is well known, and what services he has been accustomed, in return for a few coins, to render certain gentlemen of a type which exists in Germany as well as Italy. . . . Let me, therefore, recommend you to use a little more prudence in concealing the nature of your attachment to this infamous creature, who, having torn my portrait from one of my works, and having, at your instigation, written a certain epithet across it, first befouled and then nailed it to the door of the privy. . . .

" And it was you, Mr. Faulkircher, you, who ordered this favourite of yours to attack me with his stick, in the streets of Dux, at ten in the morning, on Sunday, December 11, 1791. It was an easy enterprise. Old as I am, unarmed, without even a cane, I could not resist him, and had to flee for refuge to a neighbouring house. . . .

" Shame on you, Faulkircher, shame on you ! Well may you blush, and hide your face ! "

Casanova died in 1799, and these letters were written at the beginning of 1792, about half-way through his residence at Dux. Doubtless, long before his death, he came to terms with Faulkircher. Tough though he was, the frenzy of these letters would have killed him in a year, had he tried to sustain it. Towards the close his last pleasure failed him, and he had to content himself with one meal a day. But on his death-bed he summoned up his remaining reserves of strength, and made an edifying and dignified end, in the presence of

" In love men and women for the most part dupe each other "

Count Waldstein and a number of guests and domestics. With a noble air, the Prince de Ligne narrates, he received the last sacraments, and addressing the assembled company pronounced these words : " Almighty God, and all you who witness my death, I have lived a philosopher, and I die a Christian."

PART TWO

THE SUMMING-UP

I

GENTLEMEN of the Jury, it may disconcert you a little to see the authors addressing you from the chair of the judge when, having perused their work, you may feel that their place is more properly in the dock. But such is the nature of biographical literature

In the Dock. that, while, ultimately, the author himself comes up for judgment before a jury of critics and readers, it is by his merits or faults as a judge, the quality of his judgment, that the author is judged.

Meanwhile, with the Chevalier de Seingalt still in the dock, our duty is to instruct the jury in a final summing-up of the case.

You may at once dismiss as incredible the view still held in some quarters of Casanova as an intellectual force. Mr. Guy Endore, for instance, speaks of him as having arrived independently at the most important conclusions of Pascal, Kant and Darwin. Another biographer explains quietly, as if it were only natural, that Casanova decided not to take up his residence in Weimar, being annoyed at the intellectual hegemony already established there by Goethe. The absence of any ironical comment leads one to suppose that the biographer considered Casanova's annoyance as reasonable. Schnitzler rep-

Voltaire. resents Casanova in a work of fiction called *Casanovas Heimkehr* as sitting down to harangue Voltaire in a brilliant philosophical treatise (invariably in preparation), destined to

165

blast the Frenchman's philosophy into fragments. Other biographers describe Casanova's commonplace, if not imaginary, conversations with Voltaire during his stay with the philosopher as a very close duel of wits.

Whence comes such a strange enthusiasm over gifts palpably absent? Must we conclude that these gentlemen, so impressed by Casanova's alleged wit and intellectual daring, were perhaps singularly witless themselves?

There is a contributory explanation. Throughout the nineteenth century Casanova was one of the " secret places of the heart." Men of the world, in clubs, alone could refer to him. Few could get hold of the book, and those who could lay hands on it, closed it, and went about with a mysterious air : and it was whispered that they were the initiated, the Casanova scholars, who had studied the subject in all its complexity, drunk of the well deeply. There was an air of George Moore about them, something suggestive of counterfeit emotions. These old hacks were, their manner implied, the authentic interpreters of a gay and lascivious spirit who had tasted the choicest flavour, had taken the best, where women and girls were concerned, sampling one country after another, finding each good. And since fornication as such would seem to have its cerebral limitations, since it might be inconvenient to be waylaid by a fellow member : " Look here, old chap, what did this fellow Casanova do besides——? "

they, the scholars, perforce discovered that there was
—there must be—another side to him : his intellect,
his philosophy, his literary style, and quite a number
of things—to be discovered later. Thus the legend
arose. Thus, to some extent, it persists.

It is, however, one thing to deny him greatness ;
quite another to deny him charm, versatility, ingenuity. With nothing in him, he presumed to
measure his strength with the great and famous
Voltaire ! Has he succeeded ?

Without positively being driven to it, no one, of
his own accord, in his right mind, could concede
him greatness.

On the other hand, it can scarcely be said of
Casanova that he lags behind his great contemporary
in fame.

II

Gentlemen of the Jury, you might find it difficult
to accede to Casanova's claim that he lived a philosopher and died a Christian. You may find yourselves hard put to it to discover any evidence of
philosophy in his living, or much Christian feeling
in what, after sex, seems Casanova's principal need
in life—to " revenge himself." Dismissing his
claims as a sage and a scholar, you might find it
difficult, the deeper you delve into his records and
record, to allow authenticity to any of his claims
other than that of having been born, with its
corollary of a subsequent death.

There is, however, one claim he makes that you may be disposed to credit without question—sexual precocity—on the ground that he was an Italian. There is nothing about Casanova's erotic experiences which would astonish the average Parisian or Viennese male of normal virility, except possibly as an understatement—I mean the sort of youth who receives his first erotic experience in his teens at the hands of his governess, as likely as not in the bath-room, and grows up a cynic. They could tell stories as numerous and diverting as Casanova's, of conquests at home and in foreign parts, and, since the adventures of others allow our imagination full licence to interpret such designations as " beautiful," " insanely passionate," " superb figure," " voluptuous and insatiable," in our own way, to improve on the exhausted images of our own experiences, the adventures of other men always appear to us very enviable, until they produce snapshots to supplement and intensify the impression produced by their words.

Other Men's Adventures.

"How *could* he !" we say to ourselves, our wonder, however, carrying with it a silent testimony to a feat as difficult to have performed as the lady must have been easy to secure.

Gentlemen, you may be asking yourselves in all sincerity, and to no purpose : in what wise was Casanova remarkable : what had he done to have gained such renown ? And the only reply you may be able sincerely to make is : Just in that wise that he has somehow achieved notoriety, having done nothing of note. Achieved it out of a mixture of rather poor and foolish, averagely successful kind of loving and rather better quality of cheating. That is all. And that is what you must find remarkable.

But, gentlemen, you will probably find that fraud, cheat and impostor as he was, Casanova did not cheat women, at least not the beautiful kind : he loved them and was their dupe, paid through his nose when his love was aroused, and suffered agony when they cheated him at his own game : feeling the humiliation deeply. Every one's humiliation is deepest when he is got the better of at his own job. From which you may deduce that Casanova's real vocation in life was cheating ; his recreation, women.

III

Gentlemen of the Jury, the questions you have to decide and keep separate are that if Casanova was a fraud, it does not at all follow that his love of women, too, was corrupt : as soon call his love of life a sham. For life to Casanova chiefly meant women. If Casanova produces on the whole a worthless impression, it is not because of his relations with, or treatment of, women—Goethe, Byron, Wagner, Napoleon, to mention only a few, also had numerous love affairs—but because of the paucity of the man's intellectual equipment, the fact that he was neither artist nor statesman, philosopher nor writer, soldier nor saint, but only an adventurer, one, that is, who chases everything because he possesses nothing. And he was without integrity in that sphere which more than any other reveals the central honesty of a being —in money dealings. To have lent him a pound would have meant to be swindled out of it, without his being particularly conscious of the difference. The subtle difference between borrowing and stealing is the more difficult to determine since the proof of a borrower having stolen your money recedes perpetually into the future. He may cherish an optimism you do not share, have hopes you cannot sustain, and a memory you deplore : while he bluffs himself you cannot call the bluff, and when he dies cannot blame him. Hence the extreme unwilling-

The Honest Thief. ness among friends to place funds at each other's disposal. There is, more-over, an irritating disharmony between the lender's and the borrower's conception of the services rendered. Whereas the borrower soothes himself with the idea that the money in his hands is as safe as if it lay in the bank, this idea may be largely subjective, the lender on the other hand regarding it as money lost, because the happy coincidence which would enable the borrower to repay it without discomfort he thinks may never occur except in the form of a wish-fulfilment.

Casanova appears to have chanced on singularly willing lenders. If Signor Bragadin can be said to have been possessed of any great craving in life, it was his passion for sending money to Casanova. Even when himself in reduced circumstances Signor Bragadin never mastered that passion. Madame d'Urfé did not stint her purse either. In the case of the crazy old woman, the money was a means to an end. She was securing, she thought, Casanova's services in the interests of her after-life. But Signor Bragadin, having once availed himself of Casanova's aid, thereafter went on spending himself in an orgy of goodwill to the end.

Gentlemen, you may have come to the conclusion that Casanova was generous to the women he courted—at other people's expense. If that is your conclusion you must rule out the suggestion that he was corrupt in his love. A finely wrought nature, it is true, never spends money on a woman, for fear of throwing unwarrantable doubts upon her character. But Casanova, quite insensitive in this respect, seems to owe his success with women largely to an instinctive selection of such among them as can be said to be beneath suspicion.

IV

Gentlemen, you may feel inclined to doubt a little whether Casanova's reputation as the world's greatest lover rests at all adequately on his merits— that of a man intrinsically attractive to women. The really attractive man need never go out of his way after women, or spend money on entertaining them. He need only sit quietly at home, and they will come to him. If he has discharged his trust with honour, he will, like the tradesman who has persistently " given satisfaction," retain their goodwill. If, then, love and economy are mutually interdependent, you will have to regard the extravagance of the Chevalier de Seingalt in respect of women unfavourably. Are we, then, to consider Casanova as an unsatisfactory exponent of technique ?

Gentlemen, it is painful to disillusion you, but— there is no technique.

If we examine the experts, the Don Juans and Casanovas, what do we find ? This,

Technique of Love. that if the man be truly attracted, his experience leaves him in the lurch. Whether he be Casanova or a schoolboy, it is the same. The fluttering heart, the expression of admiration, an utter feeling of sheepishness in the " hardened " Don Juan—and on the woman's side a pretence of being disillusioned at this unexpected exhibition of incompetence, a pretence which would not deceive an owl, but always deceives the infatuated Don Juan, however vast his " experience " : " Your technique is all wrong. You don't understand a woman. You are naïve." Yet, if there be any attraction in him ; if, failing attraction, there is persistence ; if the persistence be not wholly repugnant, women, being amiable creatures, will succumb in the end.

When one reads of the expressions in which a reputed expert like Casanova couched his declarations one wonders at the paucity of love's language. Darling—beloved—I adore you—I worship you. Is that what does it ? one asks oneself. And yet what else is there to say : the kiss—we use the word in its

Love's Language. most extended sense, gentlemen—is not an activity which requires expert instruction, but it does not, and it will not, cease to spell wonder while our race exists. As there is not more to be done, there is not more to be said. " Darling,"," I love you "—the magnetism of these simple words is multiplied or reduced by the person who says them.

Leaving these general considerations, it does not appear from Casanova's records that as an adept at making love he was either unfailingly successful or impervious to defeat or in any way " hardened " in love, as a criminal may be said to be hardened at his job. An invulnerable, unfeeling lover can no more succeed with women than an insensitive brute, impervious to the insults heaped on him by all the best critics, can produce imaginative literature. It is no good being " wooden " in either department. He " succeeds " who, having suffered in love, recovers, and recovering takes two or three women on the rebound, on the strength of his reputation of being capable of true feeling. Thus Byron appealed ten times more than Casanova. It is an erroneous impression that the " prince of lovers," like a world's tennis champion, is invariably victorious on all courts. He would not be a lover, that is a man tending to fall in love easily, if he were not impressionable, and being impressionable he is, so far from being hardened, easily discomfited, put out at the least sign of ill favour, prone to suffer on the slightest occasion.

After all, the process of falling in love, like the process of eating, is the same for all beings. The incessant lover only does so more often, showing thereby that experience has taught him nothing.

V

Gentlemen, we have just said that the incessant lover learns nothing from experience. He is successful by instinct, not by reason, and the moment his instinct fails him he calls upon his reason to assist him, and calls, gentlemen, in vain. You will remember that Casanova, having started off badly, could do nothing with La Charpillon. Whereas John Wilkes, a countryman of ours, having started off well with La Charpillon, continued well, and finished well. "It was towards the end of September," says Casanova, "that I first met La Charpillon, and from that day I began to die. . . ." Once you have conceded supernormal sensibility to a woman who has shown no special liking for you you cannot get right with her till after you have ceased to love her, and the supernormal sensibility will be all on your side.

You may object that excessive sensibility did not prevent Casanova kicking La Charpillon ; but you will concede that it did prevent him employing on his beloved the mechanical chair which would have placed La Charpillon wholly at his disposal.

Or you may object that Casanova's multifarious adventures were a sign of insensibility in him. It is a common error of women in regard to men known to have had a great number of love affairs that quantity must necessarily have blunted their appreciation of quality—that, in fact, these men stipulate but for one condition necessary to ensure their maximum satisfaction—that the individual in question be a woman, the one thing these men are said to lay stress on. Nothing could be more fallacious than the belief that the love of variety, of " renewal," in a man, argues a lack of discrimination, which might more justly be found in him who *Experience does not blunt.* remains contented with the woman he has. The Casanova who flits from one girl to another does not flit from any girl to any other girl, but from one whose particularity has been blunted with time and use, to a temporarily more particular woman. Getting what you want, when you have got it, is hardly better than not getting it ; and Casanova consoled himself with the thought that the strong impression La Charpillon made on him would vanish as soon as he had got her. Which, as we see, does not render the thought of not getting her any better. It is in human nature to identify life with desire. And desire with anything that may come along on a fine day in spring and lodge in your brain. And it does not follow that the man who has little experience of loving will necessarily display better taste, any more than that the man who has little experience of drinking will choose the better vintage. Any old thing may come along and identify itself with life. Consider the viciousness of falling in love with someone whom you really detest and know to be uncongenial to you. But there are stranger things than that. There is a form of vice, we understand, which manifests itself in a man conceiving a passionate interest in a woman's boot. Now it may happen that owing to the vicissitudes of fashion (or the vagaries of the Zeitgeist as expressing itself in footwear) women may cease to wear boots, expressing their personalities, so to speak, wholly in shoes. The possessor of this somewhat rarified vice, though in the meantime he may have become Prime Minister of England, distinguished himself as a man of letters, succeeded in establishing a new social order in the world, will nevertheless be haunted to his dying day by the thought that owing to a freak of fashion his real personality has been allowed but incomplete expression. Nonsense! What sensible man, you say, will bother his head about so trivial, so easily replaceable a thing as a boot? But there's

" At my age I was prepared for disloyalty in a woman "

the rub ! It is a boot he wants, not a shoe, just the same as it is Mrs. Jones he wants, not Mrs. Robinson, though to an impartial observer they may be alike as two peas. It is not, if you look round at the objects of men and women's passion, their value, but the value they have placed upon them, that racks their souls. It is the value he has placed upon La Charpillon—that of life itself—the thought of being cheated out of it, which renders Casanova what hitherto he has shown no sign of being—self-conscious. Badly placed from the start, he can never succeed with her. He tries to coax her : asks if lying down side by side would help matters. He kicks her and does other things which prove that he is not at his ease : and a man who is not at ease, a man badly started, never gets what he wants from a woman, women in this respect resembling highly-strung horses (said to resemble women), who know their riders and will not submit to a rider not at his ease.

We have suggested that Casanova demonstrated on occasion an excessive sensibility. But the evidence placed at your disposal will not, we feel, tend to convince you that his sensibility was as a whole of a high order. He appears, indeed, to have been singularly opaque in his relations with women. That painful tension between what he is and would like to be, which absorbs more finely-wrought men and places them on the defensive just when a great push would be opportune, did not trouble Casanova. Beautiful women were never in danger of thinking,

M

as they are in the case of the sensitive man who is afraid that his feelings may appear obtrusive, that they made no impression on Casanova. A thick skin, a gallant appearance, a gallant *Self-conscious-* interest in beautiful women, and the *ness in Love.* kind of elegantly superficial general knowledge of everything which women could follow and share with him, completed his equipment for success.

How different from, may we suggest, Stendhal, whose profound understanding of the process of love, exquisite sensibility, and unprepossessing appearance could only ensure his defeat. To a man of sensitive intelligence, who is conscious that the woman he loves cannot enter fully into the thoughts he finds so engrossing (because he feels at home with them) it must always seem that he is merely boring her with a superficial and therefore untrue account of the problems which occupy him, that he in fact appears to her stupid because of the lack of plausibility in his attempts to present to her journalistically, so to speak, a problem only interesting philosophically, and therefore beyond the scope of their conversation. She, on the other hand, with her free social sense, the result of her popularity, is so much better fitted than he to manipulate surface thoughts : and this is why the superior man is often tongue-tied in the company of men and women of lesser calibre. The sort of half-verities, half-platitudes they utter with such ease and apparent sincerity he would be too ashamed to compete with ; but he admires them for uttering with immunity, even with grace, inanities which he would shrink from uttering himself. He who can give such lucid expression to his minute observation of human conduct and character, now finds himself silent—a Stendhal finds himself silent, and has to be helped out by a Casanova with some banal but sufficient remark, which every one else considers a gallant act of first-aid.

It may assist you, gentlemen, in your final consideration of Casanova to glance for a few moments at the description which Stendhal, a man of superior sensibility, gives of his love for Madame Dembovski. How was this distinguished mind, enclosed, it is true, in none too handsome a form, treated by the lady he worshipped ?

Gentlemen, you may consider we are throwing our net rather widely. But it is profitable to examine at closer range the love of Stendhal before we return to Casanova. In 1820 Stendhal was in love, which, according to Mérimée, was a natural *Stendhal and* state for him. The woman he loved *Mme Dem-* was one Mathilde Dembovski, wife of a *bovski.* Polish General from whom she was separated. She lived in Milan, where she is said to have been a brilliant figure in local society. Mathilde Dembovski augmented Stendhal's jealousy by pretending that she had a lover, and when his jealousy became inconvenient she spaced out his visits to her house by two in a month. Stendhal describes the

torture he went through before each visit, how he
would look forward to the next meeting, living only
for that brief moment—the interviews she accorded
him lasting but twenty minutes. He describes how,
on the fatal day which, when it came, was one of
torture rather than felicity, he would walk to her
gate all atremble : how, once he was admitted, he
could not speak for excitement, for regret that the
minutes were fast running down, how, before he had
felt anything at all but acute anguish, the interview
was terminated with : " Till five o'clock to-day
fortnight."

There is perhaps no greater cruelty in the world,
gentlemen, than that of an indifferent woman to a
man who loves her. She has no kindness for him,
no compassion, only a strange, insane irritability.
And perhaps there is no greater mental torture than
that of a sensitive and cultivated man infatuated by a
stupid, shallow woman who speaks a different language and to whom all the qualities which endear
him to readers, will keep his name alive when she is
dead and forgotten, are dull, boring, uninteresting,
and to whom, he feels, he, a clever man, must seem
a fool.

At last, after years of such treatment, Stendhal
fled. His own account of the parting is pathetic :

" ' When will you come back ? ' she asked me.
' Never, I hope.' " There followed (he says) a last
hour of evasions and vain words. "A single word
could have altered my life. Alas, not for long. This

angelic soul (angelic, note that word, gentlemen) encased in a lovely body passed away in 1825. I could not leave her without feeling that my soul was being torn asunder. After three years of intimacy I took leave of a woman whom I adored, who loved me (note the ' loved me,' gentlemen), and who has never yielded herself to me. One day perhaps when I am old and hardened I will have the courage to speak of the years 1818, 1819, 1820, and 1821."

It is probable that Mathilde Dembovski had completely forgotten Stendhal after his flight, but all his life he cherished the memory of his love for her. It provided him with an insight into love that is not to be obtained by divination, and a sensibility refined by suffering. The scattered notes compiled by him and published, diffidently and unsuccessfully, in a little volume entitled *De L'Amour* must be accorded, after the lapse of a hundred years, a foremost place in analytical love-literature. It was fear of ridicule which prompted him to disguise the authorship and attribute it to a young Italian ostensibly dead of unrequited love. Actually, as Stendhal admits in private, it was " written in pencil at Milan on my solitary strolls while thinking of Mathilde." Though it was the author's wish to limit the edition to a hundred copies, only seventeen were sold in ten years. " I can say confidently," the publishers wrote to Stendhal, " of this book as of the sacred poems of Pompignon : they are sacred, for nobody will touch them." To a lady who complained to him that she had difficulty in securing a copy, Stendhal explained that the whole edition was now on board a vessel where it served as ballast. " What can you expect ! " he adds. " France at present is too stupid to understand me."

VI

Gentlemen, it would not be difficult to multiply examples of men of genius ill-treated at the hands of women. Consider Keats. His Fanny, to all but himself, must appear a trivial female, conscious of her power of inflicting suffering, and using her power to gratify her vanity. But to Keats she was obviously something else. Love is dangerous because it involves forces that have nothing to do with it but which finally outstrip and overshadow the initial sweet feeling which lured one. We are presented with emotions and experiences for which we never bargained. If these are of a kind we dislike, we consider we have been deceived. Then we blame the object of our passion for deceiving us. Irrationally. For she could not have guessed the real feeling she inspired in us. The charm of personality must in the nature of things remain unknown to the person who exercises it. Nor can we reasonably blame ourselves. Love is something too good to miss. At any rate, it is no worse than other things, war, speculation, for example, on which we are prepared to take a sporting chance.

Looking at it soberly, gentlemen, we cannot blame the women entirely. Strindberg, for instance, who blamed them unreservedly for all his misfortunes, gives proof of a temper which invited misfortunes to fall heavily on his head. Nevertheless, *" The Con-* he confessed somewhere that the suffer-*fessions of a* ing he endured at the hands of women *Fool."* had, owing to the expression which he gave it in literature, not only brought him fame and money but also sympathy from scores of women anxious to prove that they were different from his heroines.

How is it, nevertheless, that writers of genius, who you would think possessed superior powers of psychological discrimination, fall victims of women they do not admire, whose intelligence is beneath their notice, and who are destined to bring them nothing but misery ?

Marcel Proust, himself a genius tormented by "Albertine"—whatever her sex—supplies an answer to this question : " A woman we desire, by causing us to suffer, draws out of us a series of feelings differently profound, differently vital from those inspired in us by a man of superior intelligence who interests us."

And thus, involuntarily, while he feels that he is merely wasting his time with them, the man of genius develops faculties and aspects of life utterly unknown to him, and thus recoups himself partially, to his gratification, for there is a limit to the self-effacing altruism of a tender soul.

It is this process of recouping which discriminates the practising artist from the merely practising male. To the practising artist every new love affair is a new source of inspiration. The plain man has no such excuse. Unfaithfulness in a literary artist is

Practising Artist v. Practising Male. productive of literature ; not merely and not necessarily productive of population. Nor is it a question of how many books the writer intends to write : to create one single character the novelist has to draw perhaps on twenty different women. One may have posed for a smile, the next for an elbow, the third for the lifting of an eyebrow, and for each trait, if the author is one who does not weigh consequences, he may have paid in entanglements beyond calculation.

Having regard to the difficulties of literary composition, wives wedded to men of genius, do not step between your husband and his sources !

Nor need you imagine that love to those artists was all honey. Too often their finer nervous texture makes them a prey of their own imagination : too often do they fall victims to a fatal infatuation. Shakespeare and Mary Fitton. Keats and Fanny. "When a woman we love betrays, or a cad insults us," writes Proust, "what would we not give for it to be otherwise? But," he adds, "if so, we would not know what it was like to feel betrayed in love, what it was like to be humiliated—these would remain provinces unknown to us."

So much for the tender soul, who resigns—but not without compensation. Casanova himself, we cannot too strongly insist, was not of this type, even if we allow full credence to the episode of his love for Charlotte, whom, when too strongly tempted, he left, " glorying," he said, " in his triumph over himself."

VII

But, at least, gentlemen, Casanova was the natural male. And the natural male is a more *D. H. Law-* satisfactory product than the would-be *rence on Casa-* natural male. We mean the late D. H. *nova.* Lawrence.

" About the time he was writing *Lady Chatterley's Lover,*" says Mr. Aldous Huxley in his introduction to the volume of D. H. Lawrence's letters, " he read the Memoirs of Casanova, and was profoundly shocked."

There !

" I tried Casanova," D. H. Lawrence writes in a letter, " but he smells. One can be immoral if one likes, but one must not be a creeping, itching, fingering, inferior being, led on chiefly by a dirty sniffing kind of curiosity, without pride or clearness of soul. For me, a man must have pride, good natural inward pride. Without that, cleverness only stinks. But I will treat the battered volumes as gingerly as such *crotte* deserves."

Whether or not you consider that Casanova's pride leaves much to be desired, you may wish to examine the credentials of so vehement an accuser and acquaint yourself with D. H. Lawrence's own views on sexual pride. You may remember that D. H. Lawrence, when attacked in sufficiently similar terms for his outspokenness in *Lady Chatterley's Lover*, defended himself against the charge of obscenity in an article in which he defined obscenity as an attempt to " do dirt on sex " by connecting, he said, the sexual function with the function of evacuation, which horrified him. Yet about the same time he writes to Lady Ottoline Morrell, who had confessed to having winced a little at *Lady Chatterley* :

" If a man had been able to say to you when you were young and in love : an' if tha——, and if tha ——, I'm glad, I shouldna want a woman who couldna —— nor —— surely it would have been a liberation to you, and it would have helped to keep your heart warm."

" The law being what it is," writes Mr. Huxley in a footnote, " I have been compelled, reluctantly, to excise some words." You may feel inclined to endorse Mr. Huxley's decision without sharing his regret.

To D. H. Lawrence, you must, however, remember, sexual passion meant not the normal urgency to fit into the passing moment the love we feel to be timeless. To him it meant, Mr. Huxley says, contact with the " otherness," and with his dark god.

" And God the Father, the Inscrutable, the Unknowable, we know in the flesh, in Woman. She is the door for our in-going and our out-coming. In her we go back to the Father ; but like the witnesses of the transfiguration, blind and unconscious."

You may consider that these attempts to get one department of human life to do the work of another are analogous to Wagner's " music-dramas " or to walking on one's hands.

" The instrumentality of Wilhelm Meister's women," Mr. Huxley writes, " shocked Lawrence profoundly. . . . How bitterly," he comments, " he loathed the Wilhelm-Meisterish view *Goethe's* of love as an education, as a means to *" Good Com-* culture, a Sandow exercise for the soul ! *panions."* To *use* love in this way, consciously and deliberately, seemed to Lawrence wrong, almost a blasphemy."

Mr. Huxley quotes Lawrence as saying in this connection to a fellow-writer : " It seems to me queer that you prefer to present men chiefly—as if you cared for women not so much for what they were in themselves as for what the men saw in them." But Mr. Huxley also quotes Lawrence as saying : " It is hopeless for me to try to do anything without I have a woman at the back of me . . . Böcklin—or

somebody like him—daren't sit in a café except
with his back to the wall. I daren't sit in the world
without a woman behind me. . . . A woman that I
love sort of keeps me in direct communication with
the unknown, in which otherwise I am a bit lost."

A little instrumental, perhaps ?

Mr. Huxley writes of Lawrence : ". . . he
plunged yet deeper into the surrounding mystery,
into the dark night of that otherness whose essence
and symbol is the sexual experience."

Gentlemen, you may not regard Casanova as an
eagle, and may have no special liking for the virtuous, if tedious, young hero of what might be described as Goethe's *Good Companions*, and still prefer
Casanova's gaily-shared enjoyments and Wilhelm
Meister's moralising to Lawrence's one and only
woman, helping a lame dog over the stile into that
dark " otherness " which she does not herself enter,
during the night, or being employed as a wall to
keep his apprehensions away from his consciousness,
during the day.

What D. H. Lawrence calls " divine otherness "
and the darkness and oblivion which the embrace of
love, he says, should bring are probably a more than
normal state of weakness. Perhaps Lawrence, unlike
Casanova, did lapse precipitatedly into a state of
coma or " oblivion " : which women find so insensitive and annoying in a man. Mr. Huxley
may be rash in reading mysticism into what is
premature exhaustion.

There are many ways of getting in touch with the other world ; Yoga exercises and astral projection are possible methods : you may think, gentlemen, that sexual intercourse is not one of them.

Nor does sexual union make two beings one. None of us, however he dupes himself, can do more than *imagine* a woman he loves necessarily other than she is. Lawrence, though he thought he knew women as they were, only knew, like the rest of us, what he saw in them. You may prefer, on this question, to hear a more authentic voice. " Man," says Proust, " is the creature that cannot come forth from himself, who knows others only in himself, and who, if he asserts the contrary, lies."

Lawrence's judgment of Casanova, in the circumstances, may seem to you to carry little conviction. You may be disposed to wonder why the hale and hearty attributes of a " good mixer," commended in other fields, should carry obloquy in the field of love. Zest, versatility, variety, " joie de vivre " ; are these entirely contemptible qualities when brought to bear upon love ? Many a good man exhausts his sexual interest in conjugal union. He puts all he has into one sack, so to speak. Whether a man is justified in so employing a single woman is at least arguable. It may be an all-round advantage if he goes out of his way to find one woman for the plainer forms of intercourse, and another for more distinguished contacts. Who has decreed it shall be otherwise ?

What—but the fear of causing unreasonable pain
—requires you to be monogamists ?

If, as Arnold Bennett was wont to insist, in love a
man " gives himself " every bit as much as a woman,
then Casanova must appear as one of the most
generous of men. That, in addition, he nearly
Arnold   always paid through the nose to the
Bennett.   women to whom he thus surrendered
himself only strengthens the impression.

On the other hand, you may not feel inclined to
lend too much weight to Arnold Bennett's opinion,
who, with his meticulous habit of using time and
energy to the best advantage, might be disposed to
regard going to bed with a woman as an expenditure
perhaps not justified.

There are men who do not enjoy a sexual life,
and, being censoriously inclined, condemn it in
others, as they would condemn any other apparently
undesirable manifestation, such as spending money ;
till someone they respect convinces them that it
" helps employment "—when they, bewildered, join
a committee propagating " Spend for Employment." It does not occur to them that in sex, as in
life, he who has to spend does so without their permission, and he who has not, will not do so because
they think it good for the common weal that he
should. There is another type, as unsexual, but
inquisitive and liberally inclined, who informs himself in regard to sex as though about to practise
occultism, and finds it equally difficult to produce

manifestations. It would be unreasonable to expect
appreciation of the pleasures which variety offers
in sex from a man whose strongest physical sensation
is a sneeze.

VIII

But, Gentlemen of the Jury, you may be inclined
to regard D. H. Lawrence as a discredited witness,
and still feel far from satisfied with Casanova. Yet
even though you reject him as your ideal of man-
hood, even though you are dissatisfied with him as a
man, you may be willing to consider him as a
symbol, a kind of protest against the other extreme
in women of what he himself appears to be as a man.
You may care to contrast Casanova, who separates
sex sharply and cleanly from other
*Male
Sensibility.* interests in life, with the woman for
whom sex by itself has no existence,
while yet everything in life is contaminated
by it. You may think, by contrast, that there is
something repulsive to your fine sensibility as a
man in woman's prevalent inclination to mix
things sexual with things not sexual. It may often
have offended your man's sense of propriety
to have seen women again and again giving
unto Eros things which are God's, and unto
God things which are Eros's. Women's adoration
of the Saviour, their eager anxiety to be first among
the " Brides of the Lamb," are of that vague erotic

substance they spread, like sugary icing, over every
dish of life and which you, who like your courses
served up in rotation, kept separate, may consider
blameable.

You may be inclined to consider women as the
Indirect Sex, since they want to be gratified in a
roundabout way. You might even, if inclined to use
stronger language, call them the Unclean Sex who
cannot separate things but prefer to have everything
thrown in together into the same trough : emotion,
admiration, sensation, courtship, gifts, entertainment, dress, drink, before a general well-being

The Indirect Sex. descends on them and they call out for
the final pleasure of sex. Like pigs, to
employ an image whose aptness in this
connection deprives it of offence, they do not dis-
criminate, but rake contentedly in the rubbish heap
and sniff everywhere with their snouts for appreciation, offering you in return the table d'hôte of un-
specified feminine virtues. " What you really need
is a woman to look after you," considered so salutary
for us men, is thin fare indeed. Like most of their
virtues, this one, too, is rooted in a hunger for
appreciation. A woman at the sick-bed takes out of
you in thanks the strength you need for recovery.
Gentlemen, if we appear to you to stress unduly one
aspect of the case at the expense of another, it is in
order that you may appreciate the fastidious re-
pudiation of a Casanova divorcing sex from emotion.
For it is woman who generates the poison of the

cinema and illustrated weeklies—industries which
thrive on woman's sense of simulation, called
"romance." The impurity, the poison of it, is the
very air she breathes. The provincial cities having
no illustrated weeklies of their own, all the aspiring
women with dull, plodding husbands, whose ideas
of felicitous living are shaped by the very films
whose business it is to feed their illusions, widen their
ideas of "fashionable life" by glancing through
those hard glazed weeklies issued in London, which
give an impression of pleasure without sorrow and
life without a care. A casual collection of oddities,
imperfectly acquainted and not at their ease, are
snapped by a photographer at a meal in a restaurant,
and they become "Society." "Oh, if I could be
there, all would be well ! Life would be different ! "
She sees a picture of Noel Coward in his latest play
wearing a new design of pyjama, and she despises
her lover because he is not wearing a pyjama-suit
like Noel Coward's. Having at last promised to
give herself to her lover, she must first have the
satisfaction of having been " taken out," dined, seen
by other women—do all the things as they are done
on the screen. Then, at the end of a full day,
since the films and the novels inform her that
it is the recognised thing to do, and the best in
the land are deemed to submit themselves thus and
to enjoy it, she is content to go to bed with him, as
the last item in a programme drawn up according
to the best traditions.

N

Gentlemen, perhaps you may think there is something to be said for divorcing sex from emotion, after all, and that the spectacle of a Casanova just " amusing himself " with a woman is preferable to the attitude of, let us say, Elissa Koebel (a character in one of Margaret Kennedy's books)

Whole-hearted Loving. who declares : " I cannot. I have never been able to amuse myself, as you say. For me the passion of love must be all-devouring. It must arouse my most sacred, my deepest feelings. I require to be entirely swept away. I have nothing cynical or frivolous in my nature . . . I give all and I demand everything."

This absence of cynicism sometimes takes the form of wishing to share ideas above her head and honours she is not entitled to, because she regards her having given him " her all " as a fair bargain. Do we not know the ambitious woman who will not content herself with a lesser man than a Stalin, a Mustapha Kemal, or a Mussolini ? Nor will it content her if the fatigued great man should kiss her gratefully in recognition of the relaxation enjoyed at her hands and say, " And now, my dear, I must lay aside these sweet thoughts, and march on Rome." She will want to accompany him, share in his triumph. Whatever heights of success he achieves her possessive lust will not be appeased till he says : " This work of my life would not have been possible but for you and through you. I could not have taken Rome had it not been for you and with you ! " At these words she will utter one long, vibrant yell of satisfaction and melt into rivers of passion. "Take me, oh take me!" she screams in high, vibrating notes, drowning in an ocean of bliss.

Gentlemen, do you not prefer Casanova's incidental fooling with the nuns?

IX

Gentlemen of the Jury, we have laid before you sufficient material, we believe, to enable you to judge Casanova as an individual, to place him as a man, below those of a finer sensibility and more complex approach to life, and above those others who can claim neither the energy of the natural man, nor the emotional integrity of the artist. Our task will be complete when we have inquired into Casanova's function in relation to society as a whole. This inquiry will be facilitated, if we briefly survey the female analogue or parallel to Casanova. We *The Female* therefore beg your attention for a *Casanova.* digression whose ultimate significance will in due course be made clear. Is the female Casanova merely the male Casanova, whose sex has been changed? Let us test this supposition by outlining some of the main episodes in Casanova's life, with only such alterations as the change of sex involves.

At what age Julietta Casanova (we will call her) lost her pristine virtue, it is impossible to decide. She herself speaks of her double affair with the brothers Benito and Gabriele as her first love. She was touched by their affectionate concern, and suggested one evening that as a mark of general goodwill they should all three undress and pass the night in the same bed. Their hesitation offended her ; it showed a lack of confidence in her goodwill, she said. Besides, she continued, they were two to one. What had they to fear ? Convinced by this reasoning, they undressed and joined her in bed, where, failing to present a united front to the enemy, they were engaged singly and overcome.

The great love of Julietta Casanova's life was the man Henri. One morning, in the course of her travels, hearing a great noise in the passage outside her room in the inn where she was staying, Mlle Casanova opened her door to find out what was happening. The passage was filled with the police of the local bishop. They had come along, the innkeeper informed Mlle Casanova, to ascertain if a person, suspected to be a man, who was sharing a bedroom with a woman, was her husband.

On entering the room, says Mlle Casanova, she saw coming out of the bedclothes a fresh, laughing face, with ravishing disordered curls and a woman's bonnet pressed on a head which belonged beyond all doubt to a member of that sex without which woman would be the most miserable of animals.

Her first sight of Henri decided Julietta to join him and his matronly companion, and travel with

The Ravish-
ing Henri.

them to Parma, which she had previously learnt was their destination. "The beauty of the Frenchman had already captivated me," she writes. "The matron was sixty, if a day, and I naturally thought such a union ill assorted. . . . Vanity apart, I felt myself far better suited to him than his old Hungarian. A charming woman, certainly, but she looked her sixty years, while my twenty-three radiated from every glance I gave."

Henri was dressed as a schoolgirl with a large blue bow at the back of his head, but very entrancing, Julietta says, even in that strange costume.

After the affair with Henri had reached its mysterious conclusion, Julietta, her heart once again repaired, became involved with a couple of monks.

Julietta's first assignation with the monk M.M. was in the rooms of his mistress, for he had explained to Julietta that he was the lover of a wealthy Frenchwoman, Madame de B., a very charming lady who had no objection to his using her rooms to entertain Julietta. But at this first meeting Julietta had to content herself with the minor delights of a delicate and plentiful supper, for the monk M.M. displayed a strange reluctance to yield to her. Julietta bore this deprivation with heroic patience, consoled by his promise to visit her in her own rooms in a few days' time. To celebrate this occasion she ordered *Julietta and* a most sumptuous supper, and exquisite *the Monks.* wines, and graced her person with the finest slippers she could buy.

The second meeting answered all her hopes. " I fell into his arms, drunk with love and happiness, and during seven hours I gave him the most positive proofs of my ardour and of the sentiments he inspired in me. . . . At last the fatal bell was heard : our ecstasy had to be cut short : but before leaving my arms he lifted his arms towards heaven as if to thank his Divine Master for having emboldened him to declare his passion for me."

Some time afterwards Julietta struck up an acquaintance with the wife of the English ambassador in Venice, Mrs. Murray, " a handsome woman, very intelligent, and a great amateur of men, wine, and food. . . . This excellent *Mrs. Murray* woman soon replaced the Abbess in my *and Ancillus.* friendship, though there was this difference between them that while the Frenchwoman preferred to watch, the Englishwoman preferred to be watched." Mrs. Murray was in love with a beautiful gondolier, Ancillus, and Julietta, to oblige her friend, would sit by while Mrs. Murray was indulging in her endurance test. Ancillus, however, was in very precarious health, and died the following year. " A quarter of an hour before he rendered up his soul," Julietta records, " the British woman, overpowered by her voluptuous nature, would not

yield to the dying man's request for respite, but
insisted on exacting from him the last sacrifice on
the altar of her love."

But let us hasten on to the episode with Monsieur
Le Charpillon.

" It was towards the end of September that I first
met Le Charpillon, and from that day I began to
die. . . . He was one of those beautiful men in whom
it is difficult to find any positive flaw. His hair was
chestnut coloured, and wonderfully thick, his blue
eyes were both languishing and brilliant, his skin
faintly rosy beneath its dazzling whiteness . . . but
the exquisite sensibility one read in his appearance
was a lie. This gigolo had resolved to make me
wretched even before he met me, and told me so
as if to add to his triumph." But as she walked away
she consoled herself with the thought that the strong
impression he had made on her would vanish as
soon as she had enjoyed him—" and
Julietta and that pleasure," she murmured, " will
Le Char-
pillon. not be long delayed." One morning,
she writes, Le Charpillon visited Julietta
with one of his aunts and asked her for a hundred
guineas, a sum which would enable his aunt to prepare the Balm of Life. There would be a great sale
for it, he said, and Julietta would of course share
in the profits.

She replied that she could not give him a definite
answer until after supper. The aunt being in another
room, she felt that the moment was suitable for him

to show his gratitude for her provisional offer, but
he eluded her embrace and ran to his aunt laughing.
"·I followed him," she says, "forcing myself to
laugh, too."

When he arrived in the evening, she again tried
to embrace him, but without success, and her
vexation was not diminished during the meal.
" His hundred extravagances which would otherwise have enchanted me, only exasperated me, after
the two rebuffs I had received from him that day."

She decided not to see him any more. Three
weeks later his aunt visited her again : " My
nephew is a wild young thing," she explained ; " he
has told me everything. He loves you, but is afraid
you are not serious about him. He is in bed now
with a bad cold. Come and see him. I am sure you
will not leave dissatisfied."

Hastening along with the aunt, Julietta was taken
upstairs, and shown into a room where Le Charpillon was having a bath. Le Charpillon's modesty
took alarm, and he cried to her to go away. " My
aunt shall pay for this," he exclaimed. Julietta
suspected a demand for heavy damages from his
female protectors if she touched him. Leaving the
room, she went downstairs, and exclaimed, in answer
to the aunt's question if she were satisfied—" Yes,
I am well satisfied—at having learnt what you are,
you and your nephew. Here's your reward."

With these words she drew out a bank-note for
a hundred pounds and gave it to the aunt. Julietta

resolved to put Le Charpillon out of her mind. But
when Mlle Goudar called on her some days·later,
she weakened and sent a message·to Le Charpillon's
mother that she would give her a hundred guineas
for a night with her son. This message brought Le
Charpillon round to Julietta's rooms in tears. " You
have behaved to me as if I were the lowest of
gigolos," he sobbed.

Julietta, deeply touched, willingly agreed to a
fortnight's trial of her delicacy, during which time
she was not to solicit even a kiss. At the end of a
fortnight, which was spent in pleasure parties in
London and its environs, and cost Julietta at least
four hundred guineas, the night of her reward
arrived. The mother, after an unsuccessful attempt
to get a hundred guineas in advance, left the bridal
chamber. Julietta took Le Charpillon in her arms,
but he resisted her. Passing from love to frenzy, she
treated him " with the utmost inhumanity," but
could neither overcome his resistance nor draw a
word of protest from him. " Anger, reasoning,
reproaches, threats, tears, atrocious insults "—she
tried each in turn, without success, and at the end of
three hours flung out of the house. The remainder
of the night was passed in sleepless rage. A cup of
chocolate at daybreak proved too much for her
digestion, she was seized with a fever, and returned
to bed, where she remained some days.

After her recovery, Mademoiselle Goudar called
on her with an arm-chair, a very elaborate piece of

mechanism which placed any man who sat on it at the disposal of his mistress. But Julietta, while admiring its ingenuity, shrunk from employing it on her beloved, with whom she was soon reconciled again. He expressed his remorse at the way he had treated her, and agreed to live with her. A house at Chelsea was rented by the still hopeful Julietta, she took Le Charpillon to it, and they supped together in the highest spirits. Another night of resistance ended with a kick from the maddened Julietta which stretched her lover on the floor, bleeding profusely at the nose.

X

But the reader will have long since begun to doubt whether Julietta's conduct is in any way compatible with that of a woman, however strongly sexed. And, of course, it is not. What, then, is the nature of the female Casanova? Permit

A Cameo Biography.

us to lay before you, for your instruction, a cameo biography of a female Casanova of to-day, assembled from a number of women, like an old motor car, entirely out of spare parts, taken at different stages and ages and put together to make one Casanova woman complete.

We shall call her Julia. While at school, imitating an elder sister, Julia divides all men into " virile " and " not virile " ; and is early asked to leave school on account of the other girls on whom, the head mistress says, she exercises a detrimental influence. Her elder sister, with whom she now shares a flat, commends her to her own lovers when, out of sheer loving-kindness, she wishes to reward them, or when she cannot cope with a new man : " Oh, but my sister would adore you ! "

And the sister does ; she does everything like her elder sister—only better. When, while dancing, their men become thrilled, the sisters make secret signs to each other with their fingers behind the man's shoulder. Julia's fame spreads. There is every reason why it should do so. Let us attempt to describe her. Or, since she is a composite portrait, a girl without a face, let us parody the kind of description one meets with in popular fiction which, while leaving no distinct impression of what she really looks like, contrives to inflame the senses by a suggestive anonymity which omits the personal as it stresses the general : head, shoulders, breasts, limbs—all perfect and belonging to a girl apparently to be desired.

When, in the morning, Julia stepped out of her bath she caught a glance of herself in the long mirror and she thought, always with a fresh shock of surprise : " Am I really so lovely ! " It was as if she were looking at someone else. Her ankles were carved, as if by a loving hand, and curved into enchanting calves. She walked lightly, beautifully poised, stockingless, on high heels, seventeen, with white breasts which had just flowered, a back lightly bronzed by the sun. There was something about her face, poised on a neck which was like the stem of a drooping flower, which suggested race, an aristocratic ancestry. Her delicate, twitching nostrils denoted——.

That will do. We might add, to complete the portrait, that she is faultlessly made, rich, bearer of a noble (let us say, Hungarian) name, but completely unspoilt and quite absurdly obliging ; but, in some degree, fastidious. She didn't like, she said, perfumed men ; it seemed to her that they were attempting to neutralise some other less attractive odour.

She marries, of course, but without at all penalising her drove of men friends, though she adores, she says, her husband. On her honeymoon her very first lover, Bognor, conceals himself behind the cupboard, creeps out while her husband is in the bathroom and says : "You gave me your virginity, I must be the first to enjoy you now." She agrees. She relates this herself in a matter-of-fact tone to another lover.

"Did you let him ? "

"Of course," she replies.

"But why ? "

"Because—don't you see ?—because he was my first, my *very* first." She protests that there is no one she adores so much as her husband. But Bognor has standing rights. Wherever she may be, in Paris or London or Venice, if Bognor suddenly makes an appearance his claims must be satisfied. It is a sort of tradition.

Who is Bognor ? Just a dark young man who seduced her at the age of fifteen. He, Bognor, refused to marry her. But he was wild with her for marrying another. Such a man—apparently unreasonable—was Bognor. Always violent and straight to the point, as on that memorable hot night in June. Her father and mother had gone to bed. She slipped in her nightie into the drawing-room. The curtains were drawn. Bognor was like a flame. His nationality was unknown. She thought there were jets of fire in his nostrils. And he breathed like a horse. Julia like a flower, a drooping, crushed flower, a pink rose-bud. And Bognor—she looked round at last—apparently no sooner come than gone.

Julia tells most of these things herself to her successive lovers, again and again, and each is delighted and thinks her original.

If you told Julia that you had fallen in love with her, in fact, lost your head over her and were ready to please every one of her whims if she would only allow you to follow her in her travels, she would look at you with eyes full of alarm and plead the double danger of Bognor and her husband : " Please ! Please ! " she would wail, wringing her hands in despair. " You mustn't love me, it's terribly dangerous for us both. . . . But I'll tell you what I'll do for you," she added after a moment's consideration, " to console you : I'll sleep with you."

And she was as good as her word, stressing all the while how she adored her husband. Didn't she care for him in a more intimate way ?

" Oh, yes ! " she would exclaim with enthusiasm. " But not," she qualified, " when I have a lover. It's like bringing your own champagne to a restaurant. It's ignoble—no, there is no word for it in English. It's *moche*."

When one speaks of a woman's lovers : her first was an Italian, her second a Hungarian, her third a Frenchman, her fourth an Englishman, her fifth a Spaniard, in each case it sounds unsatisfactory. Each man reveals in love, which should be flawless, the limitations of his countrymen. To the Italian she would say : " I'm cheap to take out. I only nibble at things," and he smiled sourly. She got her French lover, a born gigolo, to take her out into the wilds of Hampstead, in a taxi, to a cocktail party. " How clever of us," she exclaims as they drive back, the meter registering eighteen and sixpence, " we've had cocktails and it cost you nothing ! " When the unsuspecting Englishman remarked casually as they sat on the Lido that the woman passing them had a good figure, Julia suddenly, without warning, slapped him hard in the face. When, in the restaurant, he barely glanced at the woman opposite, Julia threw knives and forks on the floor to mark her annoyance. If a man, unduly repulsive, made

advances to her, she looked very grave and said :
" I am sorry, but ——." Julia, said her friends, had
no business to have a mouth like that.

Almost every night in London, gentlemen, you
can observe at the hour when the theatres erupt
their crowds of playgoers, heavily occupied taxis
driving up to the grill-rooms of the chief hotels.
Among these, if you were gifted with clairvoyance,
you would detect a taxi containing Julia and
crammed with Julia's friends. Jubilant women in
evening dress, they emerge from this dark interior
and fairly dash up the steps, chatting airily, and
making for the ladies' cloak-room. But the men,
timidly settling the taxi fare, slouch in, with a hang-
dog expression. For the men, they know it in their
solar plexus : it is not the women who will part with
pound notes when the eating and drinking is over.
You may consider their hang-dog air compatible
with what, in their heart of hearts, these wretches
must feel. " Let's go to the Embassy ! " " Let's go
to the Café de Paris ! " twitter the lovelies ; and
what is more bitter, the none-too-lovelies, who
should be dumb, fall in enthusiastically with the
suggestion : " Let's, let's ! "

It's a short word, " let's," composed of few letters,
and easily uttered. Not so easy, however, to produce
eight pound notes from a note-book containing
but five.

At the other extreme, gentlemen, you would not
deny your sympathy to the young housewife who,

in the course of months and years of washing-up, expresses her wish to dance once in a while to band music, whereupon her husband or lover, ever ready, he says, to anticipate her wishes, promptly turns on the gramophone and crooks his right arm round her waist.

All day long Julia went about with a drove of men. She got so drunk that she came twice to the same cocktail party, forgetting she had been there before. " Don't take my arm, I want them to think I can walk alone "—on returning to her hotel. But she had her intellectual bias. " Yes ! " she would say, " I like him ! He only cares for sex and Beethoven, and is indifferent to everything else in the world ! " Or, " You understand nothing about Verdi. Nothing. Don't talk to me, you understand nothing ! " Or, " We'll eat spaghetti at the Taverna Medici ! " This, voiced enthusiastically, was the extent of her artistic heaven. She did not love any man but her husband, and though he hardly understood why one she apparently loved most she desired to see least, he yet enjoyed immunity from the general knowledge of his being the sole enduring dupe of her infidelities. Her lovers came and went. Each felt as if he were a parcel she had carried under her arm and dropped into the mud inadvertently.

Her household ? " Terrible ! " she sighs. " Maids leaving every week. The chauffeur, the cook, have to be bribed."

" In a fit of homesickness he returned "

Ten years of this. Julia becomes a restless traveller. It seems to her that the men at home are not worth her steel, and she travels in search of such big game as a Stalin, a Mussolini, occasionally a stubborn rebel like Abd-el-Krim.

She acquires the reputation of a man-eating woman. Actually, now she has no lovers at all—she is rapidly losing her looks, and a hungry look in her eye causes men to fight shy of her. No one ever asks her out, though she is tired of staying at home and says so repeatedly, but because they know she is wealthy they come and dine with her. Champagne, a parsimonious former lover observes, is but sparingly served. A circumstance which, contrasting with her own disdain of his half-bottle ten years ago, irritates him. He is sullen and not game for anything, it seems, but his dinner.

Where was the justice of men, she thought : in her young years to inflame her with passion, and now when, at forty, she has grown eager, lusting for it, hungry and restless, to turn their backs on her, leave her to languish alone !

At this stage, we presume, her husband dies—of chagrin ?—no, in full ignorance and in bliss, and Julia, with most of the money blown away but a sufficient sum salvaged from the wreck, sets out on her career of widowhood : to find the perfect male. Her travels and reading take her via Marseilles to North Africa—in search of whom ? A sheikh, a cave-man ? Not, however, a flea-covered nomad, or

o

a bathless cave-dwelling savage, but preferably a prince in disguise, or a new prophet in exile, a modern John the Baptist.

The sheikh, what a prospect !—a he-man subduing her by a silver-knotted whip. And he can't be stupid, or mean, or lousy, or permanently cruel. Wild he can be, as wild as he likes—but clean and generous. His cruelty was provoked through suffering caused by her wanton wickedness and unattainable beauty. As she gave him a kiss the hand which held the whip dropped, in ecstasy. And he can't be perpetually a barbarian. No, he was a disguised intellectual, a sort of Bernard Shaw grown young and beautiful, like Faust. And his holding the office of sheikh must be due to an inherent nobility, not necessarily older but at least more reputable and western than is possible for an Arab—let us say, a disguised English lord. And suddenly she understood why that book of Miss Hull's she had disdained to read was bound to be popular.

In pursuit of this ideal, Julia books a berth in a steamer of the Compagnie Transatlantique, bound for Tunis, whence she travels south by rail to a little place by the sea, but finds it, to her chagrin, a homosexual paradise—quite the wrong place, in fact. She pushes farther south ; she seeks the legendary sheikh—but *clean* and *clever*.

The Kaïd of the village, an old man to whom the guide had explained the nature of the lady's mission, rose to the occasion. He shook hands with her again and again and promised to find her a fine looking young man. " We'll find you a reliable sober man, a real gentleman."

He got her, however, not a lord or count in disguise, but one too much an Arab. He turned out to be an Arab dock labourer from Hamburg. He quite startled her with his sudden : " Sprechen Sie Deutsch ? "

So Julia in middle life settles on the dunes of Tunisia. She builds a house with a high wall and gradually acquires a whole harem of men—dusky Arabs, whom she marshals and who obey their lady's wishes.

But they rob her, gradually, of her remaining jewels—of her Hungarian heirlooms.

" How different life was," she muses, " when mother was alive ! " How different ! And, in a way, more responsible ! . . . And she settles to unburden her soul to a friend.

There was much she did not like in the Arabs. " It is difficult to write of these things," her words run. " But some of their ways of doing things make me admire us Europeans. Their way of . . . and their way of . . . and the way they . . . shocks me to the bottom of my soul, and my heart sinks, and begins to want to flee—flee away to Europe, to Europe, to Europe ! "

And like Zélide, she ends her letter :

" In a year, in two years, you will get to hear that I have grown sensible and contented . . . or that I am no more. . . ."

The Arab dock labourer from Hamburg and the village sheikh between them, and sharing a portion of the proceeds with the guide, have depleted her resources. There is a heated interview. She screams, " Enfin, c'est *fini*. Vous comprenez ? C'est *fini* ! "

When Julia got back to London it was raining and the rain leaked into the taxi through a crack in the hood. She took a room at the Strand Palace, and every one without exception who came to visit her looked round and said critically, " Very mixed." It occurred to Julia, as she watched the leading violinist—who in restaurants is also the conductor— bend and wind and twist himself into contortions, that, whereas abroad it seemed to her that such efforts of emphasis and gesture were intended to placate a reluctant public for the exploitation of it, it may well have been, as was undoubtedly the case in this non-tipping, all-too reasonable restaurant, a device to curry favour with the manager. Julia watched them : a foreign lead exhorting emotion from his orchestra ; a stolid British youth playing the violin " not having any " : giving only that which is due from him and no more, his look betraying that these foreign gestures do not help the music, which is as it is and is played as it can be. She was glad and sad to be in England. The Arab adventure was over, but money was scarce. She watched the waitresses clanging the plates and knives and apparently unaware of their heritage—

that they were a ruling race. A man from up North, who had emptied a bottle, pleased with himself and humming a little, casting a jovial eye round the room inviting others to share with him the *joie de vivre*—who weren't having any and looked glum. It occurred to Julia that just as this restaurant looked to the man from up North a place of surprises, so to the waitresses it was a place of uninspired toil. . . .

Robbed of her jewels, of her liquid credits, she takes a furnished flat off the King's Road, Chelsea. " At any rate," she now thinks, " I shall be able to write a real sheikh novel." She settles down in the furnished flat to that enterprise. The material is ample, the advice received rich, but the ability lacking, and time and energy lagging ; and the publisher's money is not forthcoming. Julia, who has travelled so much, now whenever a price asked seemed to her excessive, replied : " But, good gracious heavens ! You could travel for that from Tunis to Sousse." And she would invoke the price of shoes paid by her in Nabeul, a carpet purchased in Kairouan, and try to shame the plumber, or char-woman, or electrician.

And Julia calculates how much more cheaply and more agreeably she could live in the South of France and vacates the furnished flat off the King's Road.

When Julia took over the furnished flat from the actual tenant, he had handed it over to her with such high seriousness, such earnestness, explaining the keys and checking the inventory. And when she handed the flat back to him he had to accept it in such ignominy.

On the morning when her luggage was being carried downstairs and she was going off to Victoria and the South of France, two men suddenly entered the flat : a small bailiff of a bland, sarcastic, insinuating type, who could disarm the most hardened of debtors with a single remark ; and the chuckerout, a huge burly man ; and possessed themselves of the tenant's furniture, who was in arrears with his rent.

Julia looked at the bailiff. " This is very dramatic ! " she said.

And he smiled at her appreciatively.

Julia knew exactly what must have happened. The tenant had conspired to spirit away his furniture as soon as she had cleared away her luggage. She pictured the char upstairs informing the agent ; the agent getting in touch with the landlord ; the landlord saying to himself : " Hold on ! he wants to get away with his furniture and do me out of the rent " ; the landlord getting in touch with the authorities, putting in the bailiffs, the huge chuckerout type for brute force, and the suave and smiling and insinuating little man for the brainy side of the business.

They liked each other from the first look. He apologised for disturbing so charming and cultured a lady and told her that as bailiff he was a waste of brains ; he should have been a writer. She thought he was interesting and loquacious, a type out of Tchehov. Indeed, he told her he was of Russian-Jewish extraction. She was convinced he was head and shoulders above his fellows, cancelled her visit to Nice, and took up with him for a time.

They lived simply, a literary background making up for the ordinary inconveniences of small means. The bailiff spurned the use of taxis, which she forgave him. But when they happened to get into one of those extremely comfortable new buses, he said : " Now this is really very nice. I do like a comfortable ride," as if he was doing her proud and was trying to excuse his extravagance.

As it happened, it was the bailiff who first began to tire of Julia's society. To put it quite bluntly, one fine morning the bailiff deserted her, " did a bunk." He went off to his mother's and did not come back, and the charwoman said he was not at home when Julia called. But the bailiff hid himself in his mother's bedroom. Julia, doubting the charwoman, pulled open the bedroom door, and saw the bailiff hiding himself. He, however, jumped to his feet and said : "I don't know who is more blameable, I for deliberately lying that I am not at home when I am, or you by bursting on a man's privacy who has already once deserted you, because, as you know, I wanted to avoid explanations. In the circumstances neither you nor I ought to have his way. As I cannot apparently get you to leave the house, I will leave it myself. Good-bye," and he ran down the steps.

There followed a period with Julia of living alternately at hotels, when it annoyed her that she could not have a cup of coffee without paying a tip for it ; and in furnished rooms, when the monotony of having to wash up after herself, made her use the same cup over and over again.

And lo ! she is fifty. Her features already pose themselves for old age and she looks as if her unsatisfied feverishness was over, restful with a new beauty. But sometimes, when watching a gathering of young men, she passes her tongue over her thin lips, and says in a low, drawling voice : " That man over there . . . was my lover once—feeble, my dear." A nod. She would count them. How many had there been ? Hugo Tafler, Ezra, Berg, Magnito, Jack, Lazovski, Philip, Luigi, the Arabs, the bailiff, Nicki, and Bognor.

" Poor Luigi ! I wonder why he keeps away from me ? I think it's because he thinks I expect him to seduce me and he's afraid, poor darling, that he can't. I wouldn't mind if he couldn't. I would say to him, ' It's all right, Luigi. If you can't to-day, you may be able to to-morrow.' "

Or she would be questioned by her hostess on how she found the Arabs, and she would give one of those surly old woman's nods, " Excellent," she would say, think awhile, and then repeat, with emphasis, " Excellent."

Then comes an unexpected break in Julia's fortunes. Through a fortuitous combination of circumstances, and that accrued energy for which she no longer has an outlet, she suddenly capitalises her diffuse and uncertain interest in literature and sets up as a literary agent, without an office but with printed notepaper headed, " Literary Agency, London, Paris, and New York." Smoking a cigarette in a long holder, she interviews, prior to sailing for New York, potential clients in a cheap Bloomsbury hotel and debates the question with herself : " Shall I—is she worth it ?—secure such and such a woman author by asking her to lunch ? " In New York she would be giving parties—cocktails, for choice—in her apartment. Then she would say, " Now all come and dine with me." One would stumble down the stairs and jolt down the street, a large unwieldly crowd of people who did not know each other, to a speak-easy. There would be a publisher, a supposedly rich man whom Julia expected to settle the bill in a silent self-effacing way. But this time the rich publisher did not materialise, and an editor who turned up with his wife to have a quiet dinner at his own table resented rebelliously Julia's exhortation to join the party, and already one after another the men were deserting, slinking away quietly. Julia ran after them and told them each : " Look here, the gentlemen must settle the bill between them."

The closing down of her agency coincided with— and she said was caused by—the depression. She, however, came back to Europe by an extensive

circuitous route over tropical waters at the expense
of friends, for she was now a very popular old lady
who, everybody said, " didn't look her years."
With only a handful of women on board, she was
greatly sought after as a dancing partner by the
officers of the ship and the fat Jew boy who hit it
off with her and whose constant partner in all deck
games she remained for the rest of the voyage. She
puffed a little but tried hard not to show any sign of
fatigue, the charming old lady who didn't look her
age. " We played two sets before tea ! " she would
say, with the smile of an old lady who thinks she is
young, charming, and popular. Arrived in cold
northern waters after the tropics, " Now, for the
next six months," she says, " I will look plain."

" What a charming old lady," every one says.
" Who would think she was fifty-seven ? "

But one night in Queen's Hall during a Promen-
ade Concert she had her first shock. She saw a tall,
elderly man occupying a chair near the orchestra all
the evening, his sensibility deadened by the huge
crowd of standing men and women. Suddenly,
however, when at the close of the concert the crowd
thinned to a score or two and his own limbs were
numb from sitting, he jumped up to his feet and
began to offer his seat right and left, with much
gesture and ostentation, to the standing ladies. His
invitation was refused. Undaunted, still smiling, he
pointed with a flourish to the artist whose singing
they were all enjoying, in a gesture which implied

a friendly comment on the community of their enjoyment. It occurred to Julia that she had seen him before—but long ago ! Oh, *long* ago—when her husband, who never missed a concert in any capital, had, on arrival in London, at once taken her to the Queen's Hall. But that man, she knew now, had then been young and fair, and now was old and grey. And if he had changed, she, too, could not have escaped. She took from her bag a little mirror—and was horrified.

Then her activities suffered a swift decline. First there was professional social entertaining in Paris. Gowns at Stoke-on-Trent came next. Then interior decoration in London. A certain preservation of artistic interests. Taste maintained to the last.

Then came a solitary room in Bayswater with meals at an A.B.C. or Express Dairy, when a fluffy-haired waitress annoyed her by singing out every time she banged a plate or spoon or fork on the marble table : " Thank you very much," singing out " very much ! " The unmeaningness of it began to annoy Julia. When, two months later, Julia again visited this place the waitress, she noticed with horror, had dropped the " thank you " and now only said, as she put down a plate or fork, " Very much."

She now thought it a treat, an extravagance, if instead of going to Lyons' tea shop for a scone and a cup of hot milk she dared the more lofty precincts of Lyons' Corner House and settled down at a small table covered by a white table cloth, ordered soup, a grill, perhaps a light lager, and listened for an hour to the music. And strange, as outside in the street everything pained her, so here inside everything touched her. That she was old, that others, too, were grey-haired and wrinkled, and that the song to which she was listening was one she had heard in her distant youth, no less than because it was, like all mortal things, threadbare and corruptible, touched her, and her eyes filled. And as she sat there, very still, it seemed suddenly as if Death breathed his spell, caught them napping just as they were eating and drinking, and they, informed by a common spirit, like passengers on a liner excited at learning that they were now traversing the equator, they sat there eyes aglow with the inner knowledge that from now on everything was different : yet there they sat glued to their tables and chairs, eating, as though death had made no difference. And then a waitress crossed over to the sideboard—as if to prove that mere immortality could not alter a Nippy—and finding a fork there instead of a spoon dropped it angrily on the shelf. This was the wonderful thing about death that it left life as they knew it, merely deepening the tone : as if a street familiar in daylight had sunk into twilight and become illumined. The outward world had been slow to move, reluctant to accommodate itself to man's ever-changing desires. Now it had become fixed for ever, a shining landscape on a starry night ;

while the human spirit moved easily from twig to twig, from tree to tree, and was glad. Julia felt that unless she resisted this vision with a violent jerk of the mind, she would not know any more where to go, where she lived, and that this would be the end of her.

When she got home she seemed to herself small, sunk, shrunken ; she had to propel her frame, which had grown stiff, creaking, brittle, and peer out of this alien cover with two sorrowfully human, anxious eyes. And often, on ever so small a pretext, she felt she wanted to cry—life had offended her.

She was supported now by a distant nephew whom she had never seen and who never set eyes on her but sent her occasional cheques, and she wrote letters of thanks in which she said goodness was the real thing.

She was seventy, and each year she counted two birthdays, his and her own, and wrote to him shyly : "Well, dear, I know you will think I am being a nuisance writing to wish you many happy returns of the day—since you hate congratulations of any sort. But you have been so good to me, dear boy, and I can't refrain ; and you're the only one I've got now. Your grandpapa and grandmama would have been proud of you, I know. . . ."

Her mouth had become one thin line. She felt so unwanted and culpable, as if she had overstayed her welcome, the people in the streets, she knew, turning round to look at her hat. The crazy old woman ! . . . And all her sin had been to grow old. . . .

Long ago, just after her father's death a strange black cat came, from nowhere, it seemed, rubbed against Mother's leg and led her into the adjoining wood ; and Mother had got it into her head that the cat contained the transmigrated soul of Father, and that he had come to call her to follow him. She soon fell ill and died. And now Julia thought that if this happened again she would know her hour had struck.

She waited from day to day. One evening in the twilight of early autumn she took a stroll in the long gardens which stretched at the back of the terrace of houses in Prince's Square, where she lived.

Two black cats came and rubbed themselves against her leg, and then went. And she had to get up, irresistibly, and follow them. They went and did not come back.

And then Julia knew this was the sign. She had to go. She prepared everything. And then laid herself in her bed. Her strength began to fail her next day.

After her death, her nephew, assisted by her diaries and letters, wrote her Memoirs, under the title of *Because She Loved Much*. It had an immense sale in four continents.

XI

Gentlemen of the Jury, you will have noticed the emphasis we have laid on the difference between the male and the female Casanova, considered as individuals. Their function in relation to society, their justification, you may or may not decide, is the same. It is for them to test all the illusions of life, to undergo all its pleasures, to die exhausted and unknown, so that the millions whose existence is ordered by duty and confined by routine may, in reading the records of the Casanovas, male or female, be sustained through the toils which support the fabric of society by the vision of a rich and passionate life, which, for hope and illusion, gentlemen, are twins, they trust may one day be theirs. The Casanovas, gentlemen, lose their illusions in order that you may keep yours. Gentlemen, go and consider your verdict.

THE END